D0995739

SACRED JOURNEY

THE GANGES TO THE HIMALAYAS

DAVID HOWARD

TASCHEN

KÖLN LONDON LOS ANGELES MADRID PARIS TOKYO

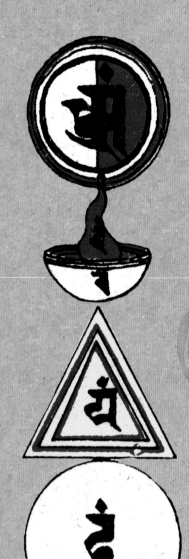

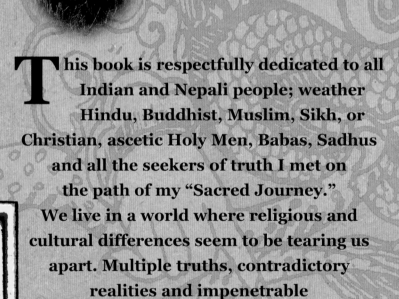

This book is respectfully dedicated to all
Indian and Nepali people; weather
Hindu, Buddhist, Muslim, Sikh, or
Christian, ascetic Holy Men, Babas, Sadhus
and all the seekers of truth I met on
the path of my "Sacred Journey."
We live in a world where religious and
cultural differences seem to be tearing us
apart. Multiple truths, contradictory
realities and impenetrable

A T I O N

cultural variations, which can co-exist on
the same plane remain unrealized and
separated, but I am confident it is possible to
transcend narrow national and fundamental
differences, accept a common vision of
enlightenment beyond all known
spiritual expression, and
follow a pilgrimage of truth
towards an understanding of
a greater cosmic power.

contents

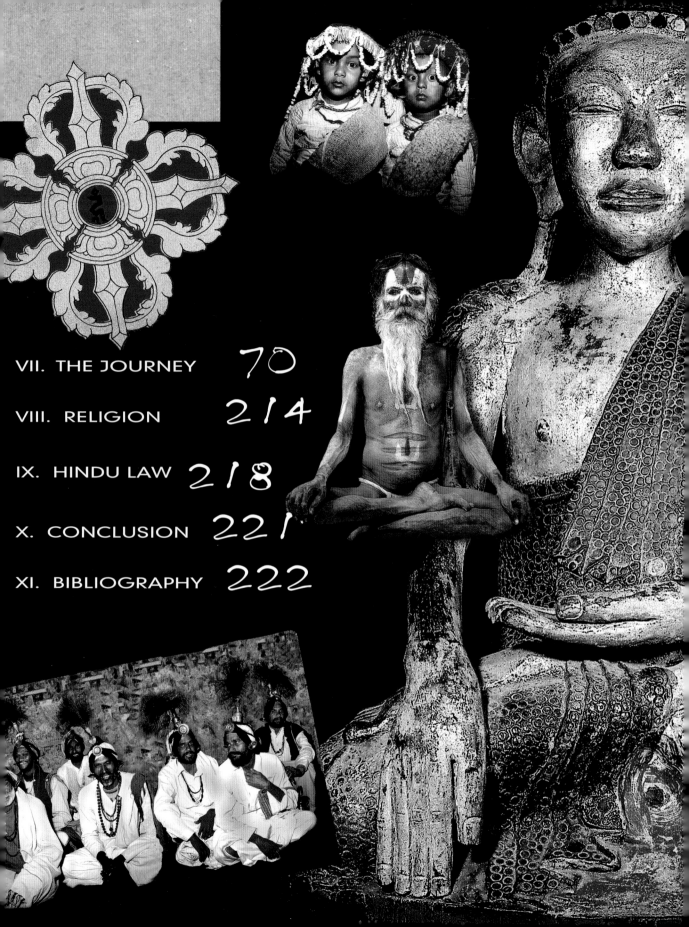

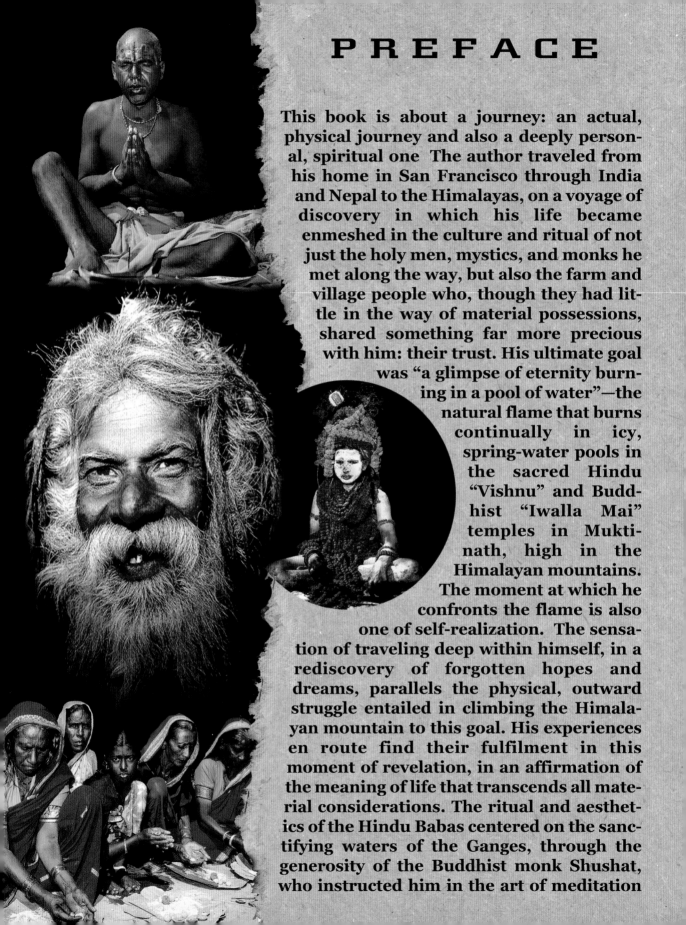

PREFACE

This book is about a journey: an actual, physical journey and also a deeply personal, spiritual one The author traveled from his home in San Francisco through India and Nepal to the Himalayas, on a voyage of discovery in which his life became enmeshed in the culture and ritual of not just the holy men, mystics, and monks he met along the way, but also the farm and village people who, though they had little in the way of material possessions, shared something far more precious with him: their trust. His ultimate goal was "a glimpse of eternity burning in a pool of water"—the natural flame that burns continually in icy, spring-water pools in the sacred Hindu "Vishnu" and Buddhist "Iwalla Mai" temples in Muktinath, high in the Himalayan mountains. The moment at which he confronts the flame is also one of self-realization. The sensation of traveling deep within himself, in a rediscovery of forgotten hopes and dreams, parallels the physical, outward struggle entailed in climbing the Himalayan mountain to this goal. His experiences en route find their fulfilment in this moment of revelation, in an affirmation of the meaning of life that transcends all material considerations. The ritual and aesthetics of the Hindu Babas centered on the sanctifying waters of the Ganges, through the generosity of the Buddhist monk Shushat, who instructed him in the art of meditation

and mantra, to the friendship of Priya, a poor woman of Kagbeni who yet shared her meager rations with him—all were deeply significant, and much of the custom, ritual, and drama of these people's lives is described in the pages that follow. With the aid of sensitive photography, in images that sometimes shock, but always enlighten, we are invited to share in this sacred journey. These are the experiences of an individual, at the heart of which is a message that yet speaks to us all—a message that affirms the fundamental truths of our human condition: life, and death, and most of all, perhaps, love.

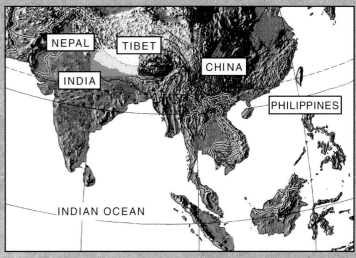

NEPAL
TIBET
INDIA
CHINA
PHILIPPINES
INDIAN OCEAN

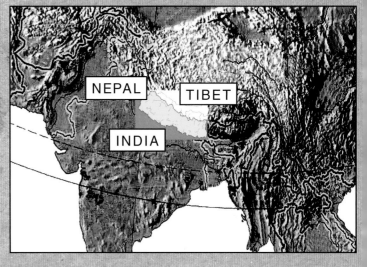

NEPAL
TIBET
INDIA

NEPAL
TIBET
MUKTINATH
INDIA
KATHMANDU
VARANASI

Himalayan mule train on route to Muktinath

Hinduism and Buddhism are distinct religions, but their histories are so intertwined they can be be viewed as inseparable. Buddhism can be considered a refinement of Hinduism, but the two faiths, which embody similar philosophical ideals and matters of belief, have had different influences.

Nepali Himalayan mountain porter near Jharkot

Rock markers on Himalayan foot paths guide Hindu and Buddhist worshippers to remote temples

Buddhism and Hinduism are related in so far as they cover the same geographical area, but a principal distinction is Buddhism was built around the teachings of a single historical figure, whereas Hinduism does not venerate any single avatar, seeing as the founder is unknown.

Buddhist "stupas" in the Himalayan Mountains shepherd pilgrims to sacred sites

Buddha, however, was of noble birth: Prince Siddhartha Gautama. His life and development as a spiritual leader form the central subject of the main Buddhist texts. He spent most of his life wandering in a search of the ultimate truths of human existence. At the end of his journey, after having observed the ways of the world and the human condition, he sank into contemplation and remained in that state for forty-nine days, until he experienced Enlightenment.

A Sadhu exhibits a "Tilaka" symbol on his forehead indicating devotion to Shiva

Hindu Holy men – Babas and Saddhus – who wander through India and Nepal and live a life of complete asceticism, on the other hand, are considered by many to be earthly representatives of God. They are sometimes even venerated as gods in their own right because of their self imposed extreme self sacrifice. Recognized through the characteristic "Tilake" painted on their foreheads, they enter a higher state of consciousness through fasting, combined with the use of hallucinatory substances, and attempt

A Baba at "Pashupatinath" cremation site on the Bagmati River in Kathmandu Nepal

to transcend reality by surrounding themselves in circles of burning cow dung, walking on glass and sleeping on beds of nails. Many employ even more extreme methods of sacrifice that include wrapping their sexual organs around swords blades or piercing their genitals with locks and bells. These rituals are designed to overcome pain in the hope of achieving spiritual enlightenment. Some holy men have even been known to walk from southern India to the hights of the Himalayan mountains in Nepal.

View from Swayambhunath

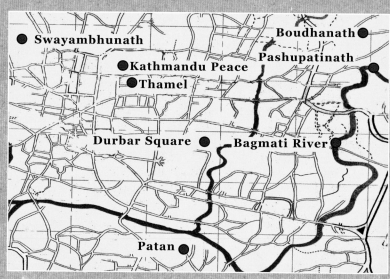

Kathmandu

Swayambhunath

Boudhanath

Kathmandu Peace

Pashupatinath

Thamel

Durbar Square

Bagmati River

Patan

Muktinath in the Himalayas

Kagbeni

Eklobhatti

Muktinath

Jharkot

Jomosom

Annapurna Mountain

Kusma

Himalayan Annapurna Mountain range Nepal

Pilgrims on the Ganges Varanasi

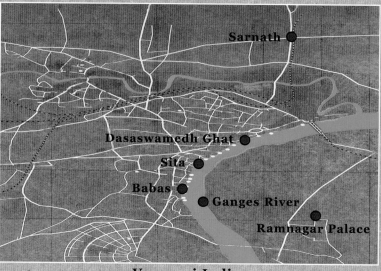

Sarnath

Dasaswamedh Ghat

Sita

Babas

Ganges River

Ramnagar Palace

Varanasi India

Thamel Kathmandu Nepal

Kagbeni in the Himalayas

Sunrise on the Ganges

Surely unique in its blend of modernity and exotic spiritualism, Kathmandu, the capital of Nepal, is home to a vast number of shrines and ancient religious artifacts that are incorporated into the Byzantine architecture. In the west, the imposing mountain range preserves a multitude of often inexplicable contradictory metaphysical beliefs. Buddhist temples can be found in remote areas with walls that are decorated with murals depicting ancient myths and legends. In the Himalayas, life is a struggle and shelter is difficult to locate away from the ceaseless howling wind and frequent snow storms. Many villagers, who live in crude drafty homes built only of mud and stone, clutch Buddhist prayer beads every morning and night praying only for some relief.
To the south, in India, Hindu pilgrims traverse enormous ancient stone walkways bordering the Ganges banks. The river itself is considered holy; weddings are celebrated along the shores affirming life while within sight cremation fires relentlessly burn. Omnipresent, chanting, Holy men that continually wander, can be heard well into the night as the exhausted worshippers retreat from the sacred waters.

Spirituality is not limited by geographic demarcations set by nation states, who could never segregate or isolate religions, philosophies or concepts as they do land mass. Hindu and Buddhist pilgrims have spilled over all physical borders and political barriers, in India and Nepal, to conquer theoretical detachment through mutual respect for the most sacred last rite.

A Hindu woman consecrates
a statue of a deity
Kathmandu Nepal

(facing page):

A Buddhist monk in Bouddhanath Temple,
Kathmandu Nepal, surrounded by the symbols:
"Ying-yang:"
(Father in the company of the mother's embrace)
"Viswa Vajra:"
(The indestructible void that destroys all evil)
"Sri Yanta:"
(The nucleus of all visible and known energy)

(below):
Two male relatives, at a
cremation, Pashupatinath
Temple, Kathmandu Nepal,
ritually dressed in white
with shaven heads

A male corpse ready for
cremation covered in flowers

(center):
Sunrise over the Ganges
Prayer wheel at Bouddhanath

(top circle):
**Bagmati River at
Pashupatinath**

(middle):
**Swaybambhunath's
stupa tower
(The Monkey Temple)**

(bottom):
**Female corpse ready for
cremation at Pashupatinath**

Cremation is the most important final ritual of passage for both Hindus and Buddhists. It marks not only a beginning but also an end to the reincarnation cycle. One's body is disposable, but the efficient purifying cremation fires assure a soul's immortality. At Pashupatinath in Nepal, on the Bagmati River, and Varanasi in India, on the Ganges, the two most sacred Hindu cremation sites in all the world, bodies of the deceased are washed and wrapped, in red cloth for females and white for males, and carried in procession led by the eldest son to the cremation fires. The ashes, and any remaining bones from the purifying fires, are placed in the rivers. Before, or immediately after cremation, the male relatives of the deceased shave their heads, dress only in white and abstain from physical contact with the living to remove impurities associated with death.

In Hindu scripture one's life is divided into four distinct, but unequal, lengths of time, called "Asramas". The first Asramas phase for a female encompasses a fascinating set of circumstances if she is considered a living virginal goddess: a "Kumari!" The responsibilities of a Kumari can be overwhelming for a young girl, but the privilege is also very exclusive. Few girls qualify. However, annual religious festivals celebrate the role of all young Hindu females as Kumaris in a broader sense; when they give themselves to God through marriage. Conceptual, but non the less compelling, the ritual establishes a young girl's tone of behavior for the rest of her life.

A Baba gives
a blessing in
Durbar Square
Kathmandu Nepal

(facing page):

Virginal Hindu girls
participate in an annual
ritual: giving themselves
to God through marriage

In contrast, the final "Asramas", or cycle of life, for a mature Hindu male is complete renunciation of all worldly possessions, including his wife and children. Throughout the ages various names have been bestowed upon these wandering ascetics: Baba, Saddhu, Sannyasin, Holy Man, with all responsibility and desire abandoned, they concentrate the remainder of their lives on merging with God.

The extraordinary history of India and Nepal is closely tied to the geography of the subcontinent. A meeting ground between the East and the West, it has always been a temptation to invaders, while at the same time its natural isolation and seductive religions allowed it to adapt to and absorb many of the foreign peoples who penetrated its mountain passes. No matter how many Persians, Greeks, Chinese, Arabs, Portuguese, British and other raiders fought and plundered their way across the land, the subcontinent's local Hindu kingdoms always survived the invasions, living out their own histories of conquest and collapse.

Hinduism (or Indiana Vedanta religion) had its origins in the Indus valley

Sadhu with ceremonial conch shell: Varanasi India

region of northwest India some time between 2500 and 1500 BC, when Vedic Aryans from Central Asia invaded this territory. The Vedic period lasted until about 500 BC. What we know of the origins of Hinduism is to be found in early Sanskrit texts, the most important of which is the Rig Veda, a set of 1028 hymns and poems written by a number of anonymous seers ("Rishi") between about 1500 and 1000 BC. There are three other important texts, the Sama, Yajur, and Atharva, which provide evidence of certain rituals. Related texts recorded during this phase include the Mantras, Brahmanas, Aranyakas, and Upanishads. The Brahmanas are priestly texts, to which the Aranyakas ("Forest Books") act as appendices.

The American Museum of Natural History # 112435
The Hearst Museum of Anthropology # 15 - 4800

Four Babas at the cremation site: "Pashupatinath"

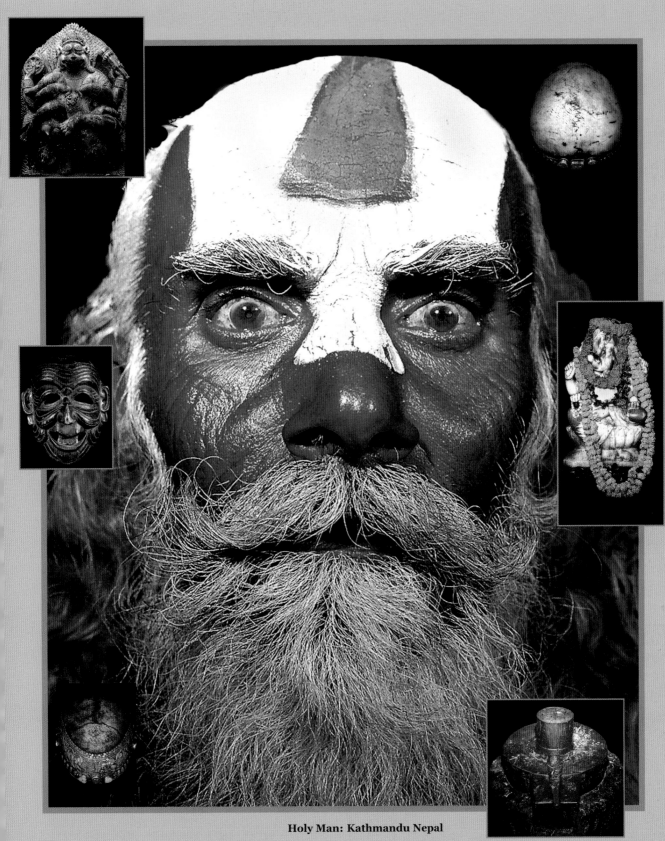

Holy Man: Kathmandu Nepal

Baba, Harishchandra Ghat, Varanasi India

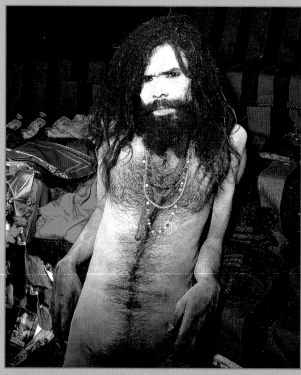

Naga Sadhu, Dasashwamedh Gaht , Varanasi

Naga Baba, Ganges River's east bank Varanasi

Holy Man, Shivala Ghat, Varanasi India

The second phase of Hindu evolution, the Sutra Period, extended from 500 through 200 BC and coincidentally this was the same period of Buddhism's advent. Buddha was born in or around the town of Kapilavastu in what is now Nepa, during the sixth century BC; his death is frequently dated 483 BC. Buddhism can be considered a reformist branch of Hinduism, but it rapidly became a dominant religion in its own right, particular-

Holy Man, Durbar Square, Kathmandu

Sadhu coverd in cremation ash, Pashupatinath

Sadhu, Durbar Square, Kathmandu Nepal

Baba, Pashupatinath Temple, Kathmandu

ly during the reign of Emperor Asoka (273 to 236 BC), though without supplanting the Vedic faith, to which most people remained true. Hinduism itself continued to evolve. The Epic Period (about 200 BC to 300 AD) saw the composition of the Ramayana and the Mahabharata (which contains the Bhagavad Gita), the Laws of Manu and the minor Upanishads.

Holy Man transcends reality in trance

Sadhu gives a blessing on the Ganges

A Baba meditates in the shadows of a ruin   **(Peter Sherman 1972)**

The Puranic Period lasted from around 300 to 750 AD, during which the Puranas were written. This was succeeded by the Darasan Period (750 to 1000 AD), which saw the development of Tantrism. The ensuing history corresponds to the Medieval and Modern periods of the West.

Buddha's teaching in encapsulated in the idea of the "Four Noble Truths" and the "Eightfold Path". Such ideas gained a following, and Buddhism spread rapidly in the years following his death, reaching a peak during the

Naga Babas: drumming and smoking hashish

Holy Man reviving a trance state

Naga Babas with wrapped testicles

Sadhus giving a blessing

third century BC under Emperor Asoka. The great council at Matale in present day Sri Lanka established a traditional Theraved school of Buddhism in 25 BC, based on the Pali texts. At the same time Mahayana Buddhism (the "Great Vehicle") was gaining ground in India. As its hold gradually weakened in India between 600 and 1000 AD, it developed branches in other bordering countries. Mahayana Buddhism spread from Korea and China to Japan, and from India to Nepal and eventually Tibet.

Mahayana literature continued to be written, translated, and studied, while the related Vajrayana and Tantra texts developed in India. Following his conversion, reputedly due to the bloodshed of war, Kanishka, Indo-Scythian King of the Kushan (circa A.D. 78–128) was instrumental in the spread of Buddhism through his empire of northern India, Afghanistan, and parts of central Asia. From there, it spread into China, principally via the monks, merchants, and other travelers who took the "Silk Road" between the two regions.

American Museum of Natural History:
"Kalighat," "Gateway Temple"
109406, 292895, 109406

The "Silk Road" through central Asia enabled monks, merchants, and other travelers to introduce the Buddhist faith into China. While other trade routes helped spread Buddhism throughout southeast Asia, it did not enter Japan until the sixth century AD. When Buddhism finally reached Tibet in 640 AD it conflicted with the indigenous Tibetan religion of Bon.

Hearst Museum of Anthropology
U.C. Berkeley "Wheel of Life" # 9-11353
American Museum of Natural History
"Varanasi, India" 1924 #254910
"Sontoli Puja Dance" 1920 Volker
"Ancient lingam" phallic symbol

Buddhism was forced underground, only to re-emerge in the eleventh century. The heads of the Gelu school of Buddhism dominated in Tibet under the leadership of the Dalai Lama until it was driven out into neighboring India by Chinese forces in the twentieth century. Under the communist regime, Buddhism all but disappeared in China during the Cultural Revolution of the 1960s.

This and facing page
all artifacts from
the collection of:

**The Hearst Museum
of Anthropology
U.C. Berkeley**

"Kapala:"
#1: human skull cap vessel with metal stand
and (#1A); cover, used in Tantric rituals. The
cup when filled with blood is known as "Asrk
Kapala" and when filled with flesh is called
"Mamsa Kapala." Deities are believed to
partake of the demon's blood and flesh
offered from within the skull bowl.
#9-1756 a+b

"Damaru:"
#2 Tantric ritual hand drum made from
two human skull caps.
#9-5151

"Dorje:"
#3 (thunder bolt) held during trance states
destroys ignorance. The dorje and bell
re inseparable ritual objects that
lead to enlightenment.
#910828 # 9-10970

"Kangling:"
#4 human thigh bone Tantic ritual
trumpet blown to drive away
evil spirits.
9-5272

"Phurpa:"
#5 (magic dart) held while
meditating ritually slays
human enemies.
9-5200

"Sankha:"
#6 the conch shell symbolizing
Vishnu when sounded indicates
a ritual is commencing
9-11952 a+b

"Prayer wheel:"
#7 exclusively Buddhist and
always bears the inscription
"OM MANI PADME HUM"
is rotated during worship.
9-10972

"Buddha statue:"
#8 Nepal   #9-8290

"Carved prayer rock:"
#9 India   #15-4800

"Buddhist prayer bell:"
#10 Tibet   #9-10970

"Strong box:"
#11 India   #9-12911

OBJECTS OF POWER

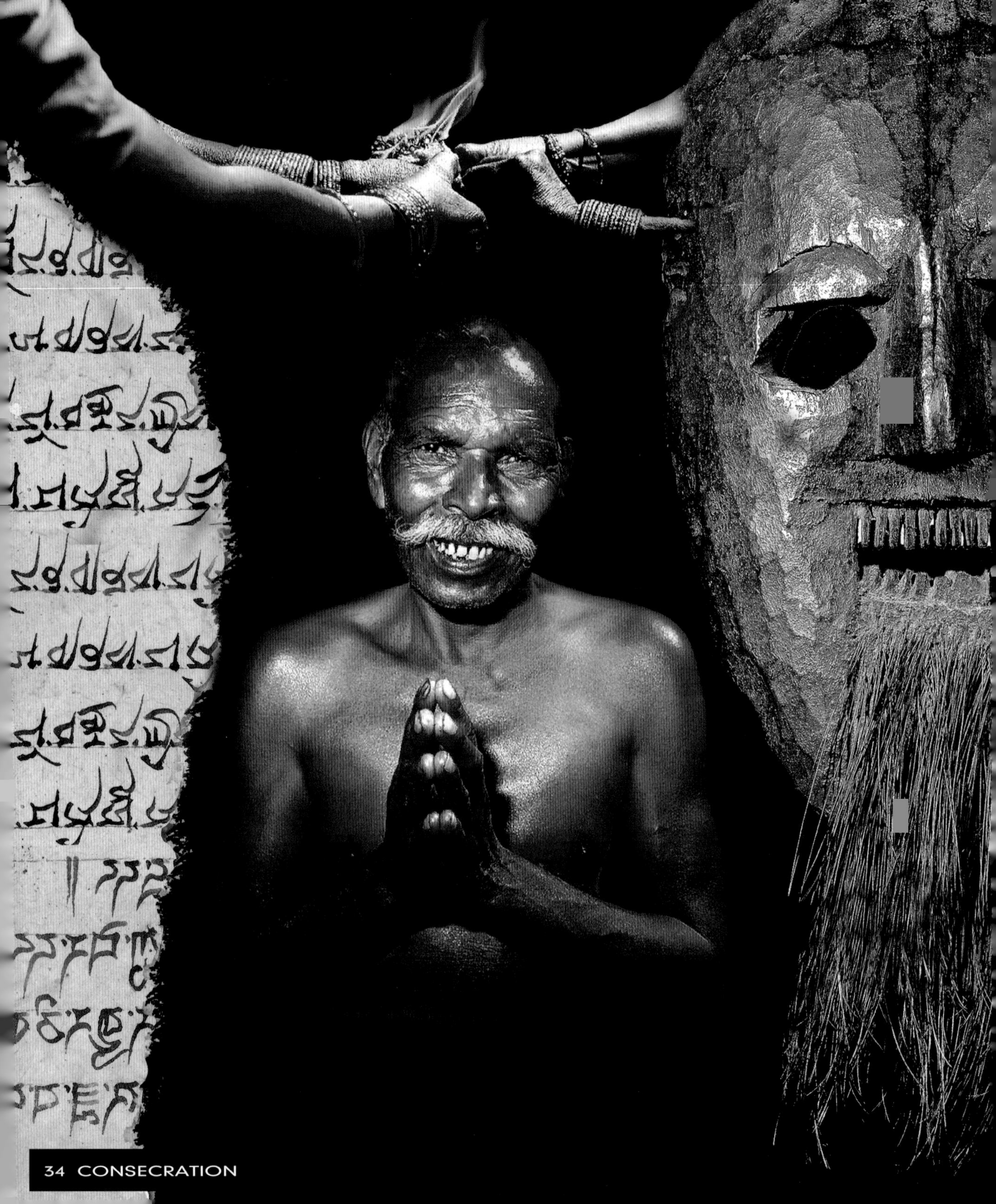

A principal tenet of the Hindu faith is that the material world is only an illusion. Everything, including God, is a creation of Brahma. It is the goal of all devout Hindus to rise above this illusion and achieve pure reality through union with Brahma. Ritual deprivation also plays an important role in a Hindu's

"Kapala:"
Buddhist
Tantric ritual
offertory vessels

(facing page):

human skull cap,
silver, turquoise, coral

(this page):

embossed copper
and white metal

conscious denial of materialism, which is personified in the religion's "Aghoris" ascetic sect, who use human skull caps as bowls for eating. This ancient ascetic Hindu tradition was later absorbed into Buddhism in the form of human skulls employed as Tantric "Kapala" offertory vessels.

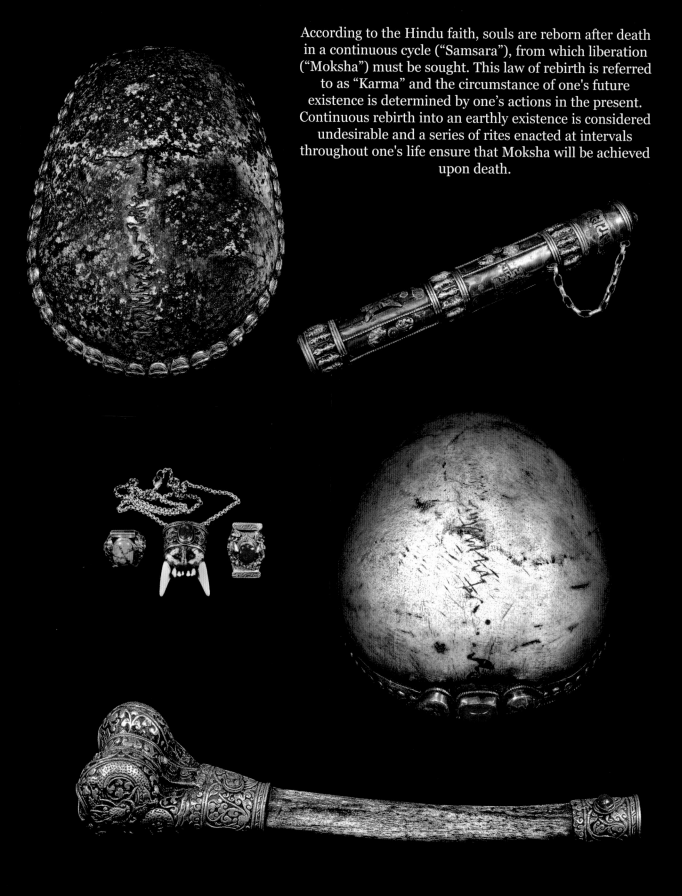

According to the Hindu faith, souls are reborn after death in a continuous cycle ("Samsara"), from which liberation ("Moksha") must be sought. This law of rebirth is referred to as "Karma" and the circumstance of one's future existence is determined by one's actions in the present. Continuous rebirth into an earthly existence is considered undesirable and a series of rites enacted at intervals throughout one's life ensure that Moksha will be achieved upon death.

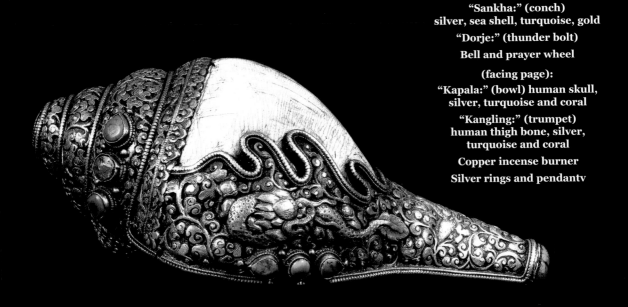

"Sankha:" (conch)
silver, sea shell, turquoise, gold

"Dorje:" (thunder bolt)

Bell and prayer wheel

(facing page):
"Kapala:" (bowl) human skull,
silver, turquoise and coral

"Kangling:" (trumpet)
human thigh bone, silver,
turquoise and coral

Copper incense burner

Silver rings and pendantv

A complex series of prescribed rites performed at specific intervals over the course of one's life time assures "Moksha". Sacred artifacts implement spiritual liberation through rituals that progressively manifest satisfactory Karma and eventually break the unwanted cycle of existence. The evolution, history, and significance of each sacred vessel is shrouded in myth and legend but their associated belief and practice is still celebrated.

In order to gain release from the continuous cycle of rebirth, it is necessary to discover the truth or ultimate reality known as "Brahman". Without definitive attributes or a manifestation, Brahman is a formless entity that is inexplicably all-knowing, all-powerful and all-pervasive. Brahman: the essence of the universe, is equated with the true Self known as "Atman" and therefore Atman is consequently "Brahman". Once Atman is realized truth is revealed and escape from the world of illusion, known as "Maya", is attained forever upon death.

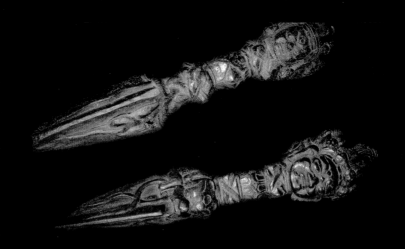

"Phurpa"
(wooden meditation darts)

"Mkshamala"
(wood and seed prayer beads)

"Pustaka"
(hand written prayer book)

(facing page):

"Damaru"
(ritual drums)

"Mkshamala"
(wooden prayer beads)

Death and rebirth can be transcended if all illusion is recognized and separated from true reality. Abstract metaphors, consciously categorizing the supreme reality, can never realize transcendence, but an unconscious indirect act of eliminating the ego, consciously practiced in the form of rituals, is the key to unlocking the Hindu and Buddhist doors to ultimate perception.

"Monpa" Buddhist monastery morality play mask from Bhutan

When Atman is recognized, the soul is freed from the cycle of rebirth.
Ritual meditation is a conscious attempt to contact Atman and find truth by delving within oneself.
In transcendental meditation, such concepts as need, feeling, emotion,

"Mahakala" Buddhist monastery mask from Tibet

thought, and awareness are "transcended" and one's true self is revealed.
Ceremonial Buddhist masks metaphorically echo the same sentiment as they shield
the true self from view.

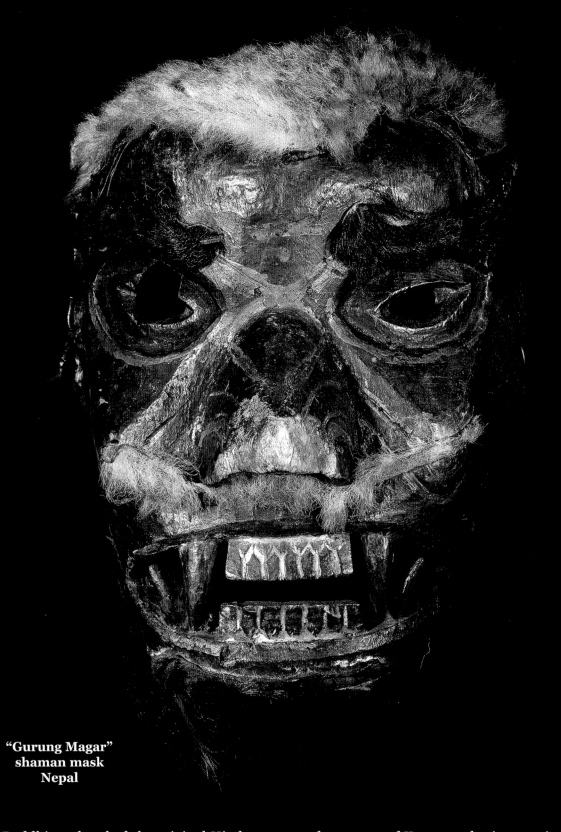

"Gurung Magar"
shaman mask
Nepal

Buddhists absorbed the original Hindu canon and concepts of Karma and reincarnation.
Buddhism, however unlike Hinduism, encourages detachment that leads to enlightenment and
liberation by focusing on an avatar: Buddha. Death, and the escape from the cycle of rebirth,
plays a significant role in both religions and Himalayan shaman masks represent a true evolution

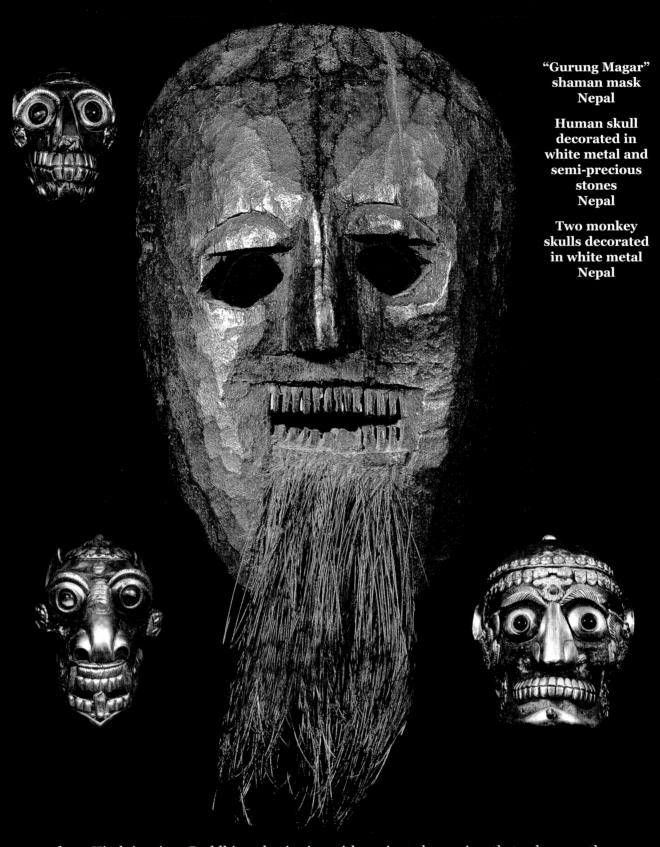

"Gurung Magar"
shaman mask
Nepal

Human skull
decorated in
white metal and
semi-precious
stones
Nepal

Two monkey
skulls decorated
in white metal
Nepal

from Hinduism into Buddhism, beginning with ancient shamanism that subsequently evolved into current Buddhist masquerade traditions. Remote Himalayan isolation further encouraged shamanistic mask making that embraced metaphysical themes and death.

1

Cham dance
morality play mask:
"Old Woman"
Bhutan
1

"Snow Leopard"
deity mask
Tibet
2

Cham drama mask
"Young Man"
Bhutan
3

2

The imagery of Tibetan
Tantric Buddhism
conveys a perspective
on death that is both
actual and metaphori-
cal, pointing up the
transience of human life
as well as the necessary
death of the ego in
achieving spiritual
transformation.

3

"Houshang"
Buddhist
Cham mask
Bhutan
4

"Garuda Gompo"
Cham character mask
Tibet
5

"Chitipati"
Lord of cremation mask
Tibet
6

4

5

One such example is the symbol of the deity "Chitipati", the lord of cremation fires, who is traditionally represented by a dramatic skull mask. This grinning, playful character often features in Cham drama, his light-hearted pranks in tension with the deeper, moral issues of these plays.

6

SPIRIT
EMBODIED

STATUES, SHRINES, ALTERS

(right top and bottom):

Patan Museum Collection
Kathmandu, Nepal

"Padmasambhaua"
(The Great Magician)
17th century
gilded bronze

"Shakyamuni"
(The Historical Buddha)
17th – 18th century
gilded bronze

(left):

Burmese Buddha
19th century gilded wood

Hinduism and Buddhism have a richer iconography
than other world religions such as Christianity and
Islam, especially in the sphere of architecture and
sculpture. Images of Buddha show him in a variety
of symbolic positions known as "Mudras."

(left top and bottom):

Patan Museum Collection
Kathmandu, Nepal

"Maitreya"
(The Buddha to Come)
18th century
gilded bronze

"Dipankar"
(The Enlightener)
12th century
gilded bronze

(right):

Burmese Buddha
19th century gilded
woodv

Within the limited Mudra classification there are many different specific literal and figurative metaphysical forms and conceptions that force the elemental Western notion of a smiling seated Buddha to be simply inadequate. Buddhist iconography is extensive and extremely complex.

(left):
Burmese Buddha
17th century
bronze

(right):
Burmese Buddha
19th century
gilded wood

All statues this and facing page are depicted in the Mudra: "Calling the Earth to Witness"

Specific iconography for Buddha had not been established during the first and second centuries BC, but surviving images after this period depict the trappings of the monastic lifestyle he adopted after his "Great Departure". Great importance is placed on the details of hairstyle, tonsure, robe and facial expression, which show the calm, smiling benevolence that most Westerners associate with Buddha.

(left):
Burmese Buddha
18th century
wood

(right):
Burmese Buddha
19th century
gilded and painted wood

(bottom):
Sino-Tibetan
18th century
bronze

Statues of Buddha that originated in the holy city of Mathura in northern India were first to depict Buddha with a round face, shaven head, and skull cap with his right shoulder exposed and robes laying in folds upon his chest.

Conversely, unlike Buddhism, Hindu iconography embraces a multitude of deities; in excess of more than two hundred, that take the form of statues known as "Murti," however these forms are only manifestations of a formless Absolute. The "Murti" portraits are believed to possess the power of the deity it represents, but the depiction is never confused with being the actual deity. Murtis must be consecrated in special "Pratistha" ceremonies before they can be used in the ultimate Hindu religious service: "Puja," and old or damaged Murti may only be disposed of in the waters of rivers or oceans.

Hindu
"Murdi:"
deity statues and shrines
from Varanasi, India's
Dasashwamedh Ghat,
the Brahman priest
"Babu Maraj" and
Shiva Temple at
Banaras Hindu
University:

"Kali"
"Ganga"
"Ganesh"

The most elaborate Hindu shrines are sited at auspicious locations, but shrines can be found almost anywhere. Open-air altars are visible at many crossroads and street corners. Such shrines are kept clean, but sometimes it is only a token gesture, as when a wet flower is used to caress the image of a deity. Major public shrines are usually maintained by self appointed volunteers who collect donations from visiting worshippers. Shrines in sacred sites deep within caves, however, are often left unattended.

All Hindu shrines this
page and facing page:
Pashupatinath
Bhaktapur
Muktinath
Patan
Kathmandu
Nepal

To prevent theft and destruction to Hindu shrines and monuments cast metal and carved stone have been the elements of choice. Hindu altars decorate entire regions within southeast Asia, although nothing is specifically known about the artists, craftsmen, or even the founder of the Hindu religion; it has continued to exist for thousands of years as an ununified system of ideas and practice that cannot be confined to a Western definition of religion.

The great Hindu God "Shiva" takes an anthropomorphic form but he is also embodied in the powerful image of the "lingam." A phallic symbol, the lingam represents the power of the cosmos and is kept away from the shrines of other deities. Because of the importance and power in the mystery of Shiva as a deity, his symbol is usually only found at temples. Although phallic, this image should not be confused with having a sexual connota-

tion. It represents the necessary energy for life in our physical realm, as well as the life of the entire cosmos being as one. Shiva, when not symbolized by the lingam, can be recognized by the horizontal "tilaka" markings on his forehead, and his blue throat stained by the poison he consumed as savior of the world which signifies: what dies must be reborn.

(this page):
**All Hindu
"Shiva Lingam"
shrines**

(facing page bottom):
"Shiva Lingam"

(facing page top):
**Shrouded Hindu
deity statues**

The Hindu deity: "Sahasrabhuja Avalokiteswara"
Symbols play an important part in both Hinduism and Buddhism. Each inexplicable metaphysical or intangible religious concept is given a physical presence, which embodies, and is represented by, a symbol that is impossible to communicate in any form.

Symbolizing the universe: "Mandalas" are circular graphic visual aids used to stimulate the concentration and introspective meditation designed to activate the "Siddi" force within the universe.

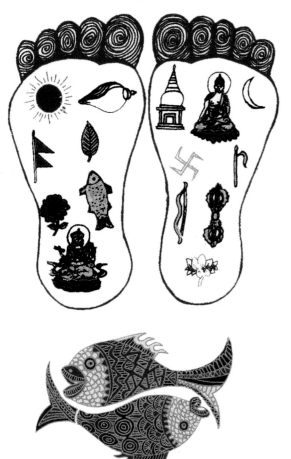

(facing page clockwise from top left):

Om, Yantra, Buddha's Eyes, Buddha's Hands, Suvarna Matsya, Buddha's feet

(this page clockwise from top left):

Mandala, Double Dorje, Poorna Kalash, Ying-Yang (Yab-Yum)

The most sacred symbol for both Hindus and Buddhists, "OM" is composed of three Sanskrit letters and represents everything in the cosmos that is manifest ("Saguna") and hidden ("Nirguna.") "OM" is universal and, although it is impossible to define, it remains a symbol that represents everything that exists.

Hindu pilgrims
on the Ganges
Varanasi India

After three decades of travel and self-discovery I found myself at the very same place I had started from. It was not wasted time, because on this "sacred trek" I not only renewed philosophical values I had abandoned more than thirty years earlier, but I also found myself reaffirming aesthetic and spiritual priorities I had learned, and then forgotten, over the course of a lifetime.

From San Francisco, the odyssey carried me to Tokyo, Bangkok, Kathmandu, and finally India. The four exhausting flights took more than twenty hours in the air, plus an additional twelve in lay-overs. It took only thirty-six hours to go halfway around the globe, but the time zones, jet lag, airplane food and the connections from California's high tech Silicon Valley to the medieval surroundings of India, guaranteed my complete disorientation upon arrival.

Varanasi, India, on the Ganges River

I was devastated by the stark contrast between the two sides of the world. The last flight brought me to Varanasi, the place in India where the ashes of Jerry Garcia and George Harrison were scattered upon the sacred waters of the Ganges. When I reached the banks and first glimpsed the spectacle of ageless Hindu rituals, an exhilarating, almost inexplicable sensation took possession of my being. The feeling was flickering, archetypal.

It was a pleasant separation from my normal rational self. I was determined to bathe in and absorb the new perception. As I let it wash over me I felt it purify my spirit. But before I would sense this inexplicable experience I first had to travel from the diminutive Varanasi airport to the banks of the river, a short and, I had imagined, routine trip of only twenty miles. I felt like instead of seeing reality, I was watching a movie reflected in a glass tabletop.

Fear swept over me as I exited the airport and was surrounded by a large group of shouting men. Their accents were so thick I could not tell at first what they were screaming, but soon realized they were taxi drivers, extremely willing to take me wherever I wanted to go.

Some wore turbans with western-style suits and ties, while others sported odd mixes of attire from every part of the globe. I bargained quickly to get the best possible fare to the river but remained overwhelmed by the strange temperament and dress of the drivers. "Honesty is the best policy! I am Vinodh, and your name is...?" one queried. Responding to the suggestion of honesty made me feel slightly uncomfortable. Digesting the cliché was not the problem, but whenever I meet a stranger professing "friendship" or "honesty," the overture usually precedes some form of treachery. I reluctantly accepted his offer as I kept a close eye on my valuables located in the side pocket of my backpack. The traffic progressively thickened the closer we got to the Ganges. Finally, when we were within a few blocks of the river, a policeman in the roadway raised a single white-gloved

Hindu pilgrims practice fire rituals and bathe in the sanctifying waters of the Ganges

hand and stopped our progress. He approached the cab speaking in Hindi. Vinodh translated: "The streets are blocked, closed to all traffic. From here to the river we must go on foot." On the opposite side of the jammed intersection, beyond a bamboo barrier, there were no motorized vehicles, while donkey carts, rickshaws, bicycles and pedestrians filled the roadway and overflowed onto the sidewalks. As we got out of the car, Vinodh grabbed my backpack and slipped it over his shoulder. My suspicion subsided only when I realized the sheer weight of the bag made it impossible for him to outrun me. I followed him as he maneuvered under the - makeshift wooden roadblock but lost sight of him when he disappeared down an alley only yards in front of me. Panicked, I ran to catch up with him, but my fears were unfounded: the alley was the only possible way to get down to the river. The narrow cobblestone walkway divided and subdivided into a labyrinth of catacomb passages filled with the excrement of freely roaming cows. The air was pungent with a burning odor from men urinating only inches from women washing dishes in water drawn from wells at the alley's intersections. Muslim women, covered in robes from head to foot, with only slits revealing their eyes, carried torches that provided the only illumination as the day turned to dusk. I could never have found my way through the dim, zig-zagging complex of alleys without Vinodh. Suddenly he stopped and rapped on an enormous wooden double door with an oversized brass knocker.

I was relieved to read the name emblazoned above the threshold:

Vishnu Rest House.

My fear turned to profound gratitude and I attempted to conceal my embarrassment. Vinodh truly was an honest man. The proprietor emerged, holding a candle, and broke the bad news to me: No vacancies.

Apparently everyone else read the same guide books I had, which proclaimed the Vishnu the best guesthouse on the Ganges. It was now dark and impossible to see as I stumbled through the snaking stone walkways. My heart jumped when I heard the sound of gunfire. Drunken revelers carrying old, wooden, single-shot bolt-action rifles paraded past us toting an effigy. Vinodh said it was an annual pilgrimage of students on their way to deposit the Hindu deity statue into the sacred river. But concern for shelter was my priority. I needed to rest, but where? Then I remembered, a friend back in California had visited Varanasi a decade earlier, and suggested I go to the inviting, albeit dilapidated and monkey-infested, accommodations he had

found. What did he say was the name of that place? "Vinodh, do you know how to get to the Sita?"

His response was a reassuring nod. Without a word he turned back into the darkness of the ally from which we had just emerged. Dreading being stranded without my trustworthy guide, I struggled to keep up with him as we retraced our steps through the confusing tunnels and twisting pathways. Within minutes we arrived at the threshold of the Sita. Expecting to see a deteriorating facade, I was delighted to discover that the guesthouse had undergone a complete renovation since my friend had visited. I do not remember falling asleep, but the next day I awoke at dawn as sunlight streaked across the Ganges into my bedroom's balcony window. I got up and ran down to the banks with my camera.

The spiritual enclave was already inhabited by practitioners of countless persuasions, who were immersed in the sacred river performing a variety of rituals. Two women embracing a burning sacrifice slipped into the brisk water. Some crossed their hands and held them reverently over their chests as they entered the Ganges. Others, praying with closed eyes, dipped in the water as the sun peeked over the horizon and warmed the worshippers.

Seven women prepared food on enormous stone blocks that lined the river's banks. A family member had died and their rations ensured the deceased sustenance in the next life. Five women bathed together in the holy water while holding each other's wet clothing. Some devotees poured buckets of sacred water back into the Ganges as they prayed. Submerged worshippers were oblivious to everything except spiritual rejuvenation as their bodies came in contact with the sanctifying liquid. Above the holly river, with folded hands, one closed-eyed pilgrim floated only on faith.

As women ritually prepared food at dawn for the dead, worshippers prayed while bathing in the Ganges

I had decided to come to the Ganges because the Hindu festival of Kumbha Mela was in progress at the intersection of three rivers only one hundred kilometers from Varanasi. The climax of Kumbha Mela is when congregations of holy men, known as sadhus or babas, are followed by Hindu devotees to the sacred waters at dawn. The holy men, who passed through Varanasi to and from the festival, became the focus of my journey through India and into the Himalayan Mountains of Nepal. I befriended many babas on my journey and learned about their ascetic sacrifices, their perpetual consumption of hashish, and their meditation-induced trance states.

An old and a young baba on the banks of the Ganges, Varanasi

But as of yet, I hadn't even seen one. It was only my first day, in what I considered the most sacred place on earth. I had thought there was a chance to find God, or at least the closest thing to God, but as I wandered south on the banks of the Ganges I began questioning my quest. Was I being too ambitious or unrealistic, hoping against all odds to find some kind of burning bush? I had started to lose faith, and question even the very existence of God, when I happened upon hundreds of nomadic babas camped on both sides of the river. Smoke rose from their tents and their bamboo lean-tos covered with blue plastic tarps. I was attracted to a red and white design on a baba's forehead, and my interest was not unnoticed.

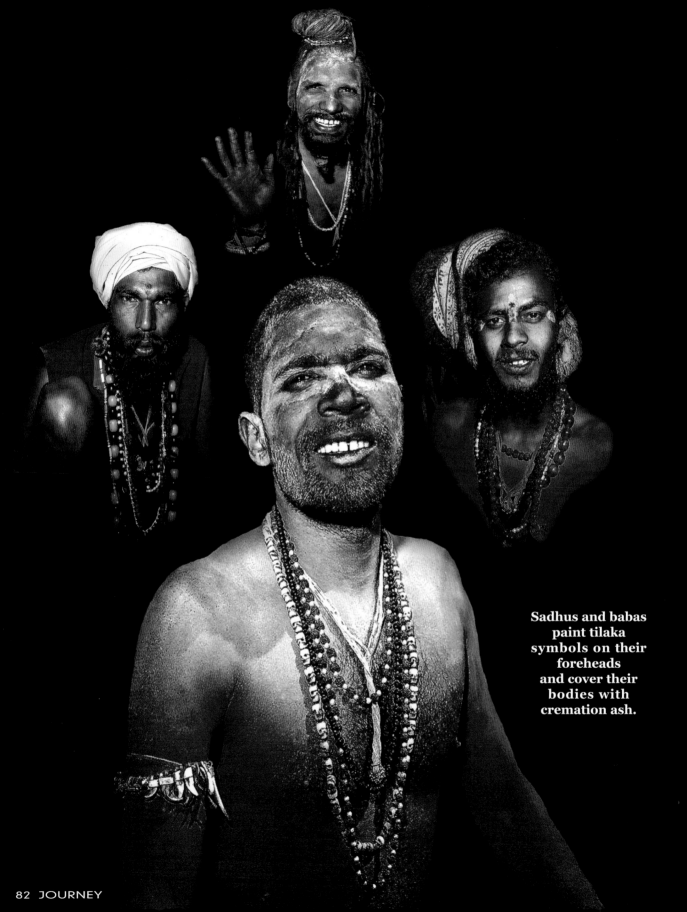

Sadhus and babas
paint tilaka
symbols on their
foreheads
and cover their
bodies with
cremation ash.

The mark on the sadhu's forehead was the first symbolic identification of a holy man I had seen. I soon became entranced, and for the next six hours was immobile, while the baba utilized what seemed like thousands of hand signals, along with broken English, to explain that the tilaka carefully painted on his forehead denoted a sectarian affiliation and symbolized the philosophy of his faith. The trident design ignifies reverence and worship of Lord Shiva, he explained, and Shiva's canon dictates that his followers must reside at cremation ghats.

He explained that a ghat is a sacred place along the river where the bodies of the dead are brought, ritually dressed, blessed, and then cremated by their loved ones. I looked at the pale powder that was part of his tilaka. Without my having to ask, he said, "This? This is ash from cremation fire." I later learned that some babas cover their entire bodies in cremation ash. After several more hours of smoking, drinking tea and talking, I got up and started moving in the direction of the tent flap opening.

The baba with the
Shiva trident tilaka

(facing page):

A novice sadhu wearing
cremation ash.

The sadhu signaled me to stay, and, handing me the cups we had been drinking from, said, "Go wash in river." I understood this was part of my training, to be relegated to a subservient position, but now I realized he assumed my communication with him was a request to follow and be taught his ascetic secrets. I willingly washed our cups in the Ganges and returned to his tent, presuming our encounter would now end, but again he petitioned me to enter his domain. As I sat cross-legged in a lotus position on the floor of his lean-to, he took my head in both his hands and gently guided it forward down to the ground. Suddenly he slapped the middle of my back, directly on the spine, with an open palm. The sound was extremely loud, but there was very little pain. He then put the thumb of his right hand into the ashen remains of an extinguished fire at the entrance of his tent and smeared it onto my forehead between my eyes.

Naga sadhus, known as warrior ascetics, wear no clothes and have existed since time immemorial

He placed a necklace, made from a brown seed strung on a black thread, over my head. I felt honored, but being accepted was even more important. We bowed to each other and in silence separated forever.

The sun started to set on my first day in Varanasi as I trekked north along the banks of the Ganges back to the Sita Guest House. While climbing the gigantic stone steps that led up from the river, I heard a low moan coming from the shadows: "Baba ... Baba ... Baba ..." The three repeated words, a pause, and then the three words, over and over again like a mantra. There was a brief silence, then the haunting cry sounded again. The cadence was slower, but now more deliberate. I cautiously approached the darkness, and there, in an alcove reserved for debris, was the outline of a human form. I penetrated deeper into the shadows, and behind a brick wall that surrounded the enclosure, I discovered a disabled man soaking in a pool of his own urine, begging for food.

I took a plastic bottle of drinking water from my camera bag, stripped off my T-shirt, and poured some of the liquid onto the cloth. I cleaned the beggar's loins of urine and in the darkness repositioned him on a dry spot. I gave him what I could spare: sixty Indian rupees, the equivalent of one and a half U.S. dollars, and handed him some crackers I always keep tucked away in my shirt's front pocket. I felt ashamed offering the meager meal, and such a small amount of money, but what more could I have done?

An endless supply of beggars line the banks of the Ganges as pilgrims perform religious incantations

Semi-precious talisman jewelry, a Sanskrit text, and hands painted red with mahendi (henna)

The sound of brahmins calling devotees to the Ganges lured me out of a sleepy jet-lagged delirium as I rose the next morning. Beautiful golden light reflected off the river, while large wooden row-boats loaded with Hindu pilgrims maneuvered in every conceivable direction, hoping to beat the uncomfortable midday heat. As I descended the steep stone stairway to the Ganges I caught sight of the brahmins sitting under their enormous, tattered, bamboo and palm frond umbrellas, which outlined the contour of the river bank.

Some wore
several layers of
inexpensive gaudy
jewelry, while others
had red mahendi
designs painted
on their hands.
I inquired if the
symbols and gems
had any meaning
and was told that
semi-precious
stones are Hindu
talismans used to
elicit beneficial
spiritual
rewards.

Before any
further explanation
was possible,
a completely nude
baba passed me,
walking in the
general direction
of the largest
cremation ghat.
He was nude except
for a large brass
bell attached to an
oversized steel
padlock threaded
through a hole
in his penis.

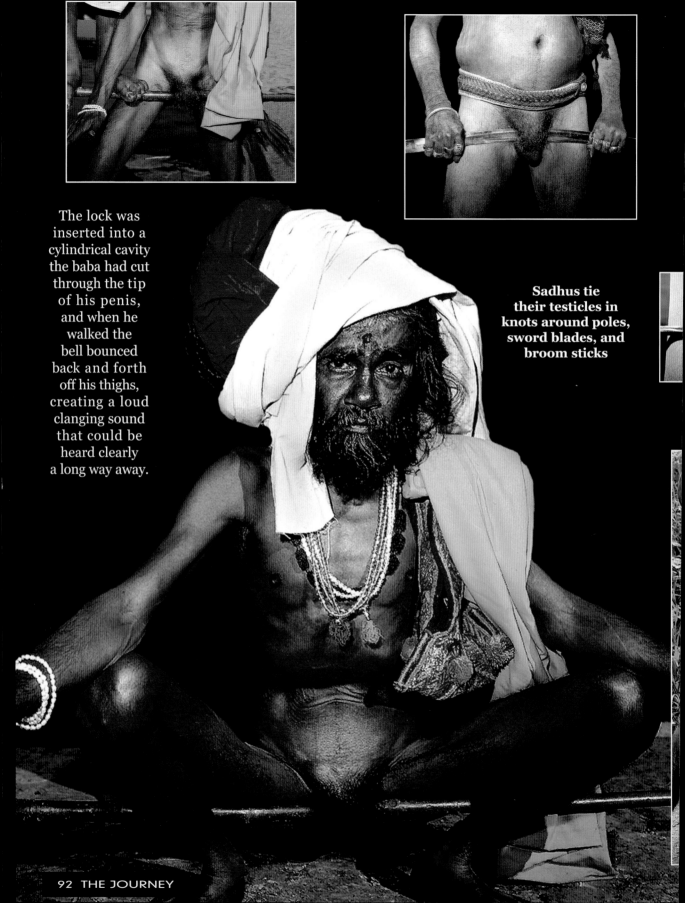

The lock was inserted into a cylindrical cavity the baba had cut through the tip of his penis, and when he walked the bell bounced back and forth off his thighs, creating a loud clanging sound that could be heard clearly a long way away.

Sadhus tie their testicles in knots around poles, sword blades, and broom sticks

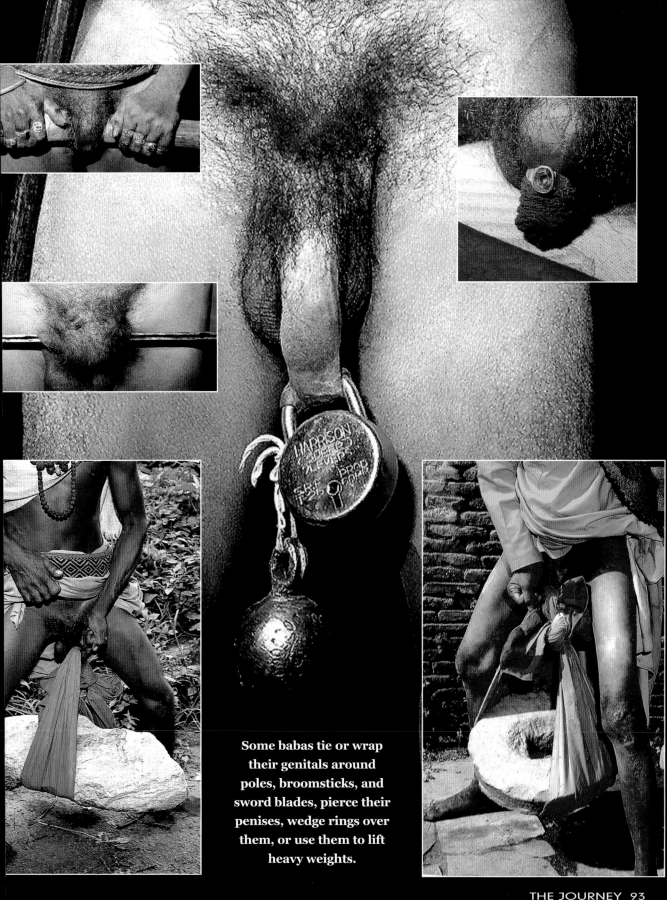

Some babas tie or wrap their genitals around poles, broomsticks, and sword blades, pierce their penises, wedge rings over them, or use them to lift heavy weights.

The sound of the baba's bell receded into a cacophony that emanated from the largest cremation ghat. As the holy man's nude torso vanished into a large oncoming crowd of pilgrims, a sound like a blaring trumpet replaced the clanging of his bell. I inched forward as far as could through the surrounding mob, but I couldn't get close enough to see the source of the sound.

Jangama babas and snake charmers on the banks of the Ganges River Varanasi India

A plaintive wail emanated from a flutelike instrument made from a gourd. A snake charmerwas playing to entice cobras. This was the source of the sound I had heard. When I reached a vantage point from where I could see, high-pitched screams suddenly rose from a nearby Muslim woman. Her young son had come too close to one of the snakes.

**Varanasi India
and
(top right):
Kathmandu: silver
armband in the form
of a snakelike om**

I never learned whether
he lived or died, but
from that moment on
I always approached
the charmers' pets
with extreme caution.
I recall this unfortunate
incident frequently
and unwillingly.
No matter how hard
I try, I can never
forgetting the
brutal punishment
given to that
helpless street
performer.

The serpent's fangs
penetrated the
boy's right index
finger. Although still
juvenile, the cobra was
nonetheless potentially
lethal. The boy was
rushed to the hospital.
I later learned he
became seriously ill.
But before the mob
determined the child's
condition, revenge was
swiftly meted out.
A baseball-sized stone
struck the right temple
of the snake charmer's
head, then a hail of
stones flew in his
direction. Soon the
reptiles' minstrel lay
unconscious, his body
a motionless heap
of indistinct flesh.

Dasashwameth. I wanted to capture
candid shots of typical Hindu marriages
and this is the ceremonies' center where
an endless stream of marriage rituals
are performed nonstop. But I quickly
discovered my camera's focal length
was far too short to make any successful
telephoto exposures. It was necessary
to move within the intimate
space of the actual rituals
which required permission
So I begged, gesturing at the
Hasselblad strapped around
my neck. They could not
speak a word of English
but they divined my
intent. The entire
party was helpful
and gregarious
as the celebrants
assisted me by
making way

Legend has it that before Hindu
women are permitted to marry
they must kiss the head of a
cobra three times to prove
their love to their betrothed.
Varanasi is not only a venue for
snake charmers, it is also the
most auspicious place for
marriage throughout all
of India. Late in the
afternoon, on my
fifth day in Varanasi,
I surreptitiously
selected a
hiding place
within the
main
ghat,

I was able to gain access to the most advantageous location to photograph their wedding ritual, which was with ▮▮▮ck to the sun, while standing knee-deep in the Ganges. The party encouraged me to photograph the red mahendi-decorated bare feet of the groom and hands of the bride. Some of the brides, tethered on leashes made of elaborate colored cloth, trailed behind their soon-to-be husbands. Others wore large golden rings in pierced nostrils and glistening medallions fashioned to the center of their foreheads. Some were completely covered in ▮himmering golden gowns, obscuring their facial features, while the grooms boasted intricately

flowered red and gold beaded crowns. The ceremony ended with an abrupt charge onto a waiting multi-tiered boat. As musicians played, the vessel swiftly crossed the great Ganges and reached privacy on the far bank.

Hindu groom, Kathmandu, Nepal

Groom's mahendi-decorated feet, Varanasi

(facing page):

Hindu bride on the Ganges

Bride's mahendi-decorated hands, Varanasi

The wedding party's hospitality and the ritual were unforgettable. And as the gods would have it, I stumbled upon an even more remarkable Hindu ceremony at the very same location, though I would have to wait until nightfall before it would begin.

Brides, Varanasi

Wedding party on the Ganges

Wedding car, Kathmandu

(facing page):

Marriage ceremony on the Ganges

Brides tethered on leashes, Varanasi

I had the unexpected opportunity to participate in another sanctification. This time it was the most sacred of all Hindu rituals, puja, and fate was surely smiling, because the ceremony was presided over by a well-known brahmin priest, Babu Maraj.

During the day Dasashwameth ghat is a marketplace and
marriage site, but at night it is magically transformed.
A magnificent altar was subtly illuminated for the ritual,
beautifully adorned with flowers, candles, incense, and
the ceremonial implements of puja, within only a
few feet of the water of the Ganges .

**Babu Maraj, the brahmin
priest, blesses the faithful**

**The essential puja implements,
kaporrarti and jhararti,
hold the sacred fires offered
over the Ganges. Chawor,
the lily-white ritual hair whisk,
assures spiritual cleanliness.**

As daylight waned, the sun sank below the horizon, and a brilliant glow from a rising full moon was mirrored perfectly in the Ganges. Where the light fell off into darkness, a charismatic figure arose. His indistinct form progressively materialized as he reverently approached the altar.

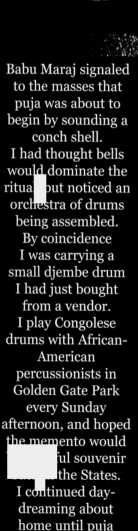

Babu Maraj signaled to the masses that puja was about to begin by sounding a conch shell.

I had thought bells would dominate the ritual, but noticed an orchestra of drums being assembled.

By coincidence I was carrying a small djembe drum I had just bought from a vendor.

I play Congolese drums with African-American percussionists in Golden Gate Park every Sunday afternoon, and hoped the memento would ████████ souvenir ████████ the States.

I continued daydreaming about home until puja brought me to my senses when it began with a thundering combination of drums, bells, and flutes. Familiar with drumming, I longed to join the ensemble, but did not want to participate if I was unwelcome. My compromise was to play only during the crescendos.

Immediately after my first contribution the lead drummer raised his head and made eye contact with me, even though I was in the last row of the congregation.

I thought he wanted me to stop, but on the contrary

he was delighted, and waved me down to join the band. I pounded my tiny drum with enthusiastic abandonment and inadvertently slipped into a trance. How long it lasted I will never know. After returning to the guest house, while regaining normal consciousness, I urinated a continuous stream of scarlet blood. I still revel in the fact I had participated, although unwittingly, in my very first blood sacrifice. Even today I vividly see,

in my mind's eye, Babu Maraj holding the flame high above his ███, then down within inches of the Ganges, as its brilliant beams of blinding light joined the moon's reflection in the river. The blood I let was a small price to pay for such a rewarding

and unforgettable cathartic experience which would surely mold my character forever, from the moment I first saw the sacrificial guiding light, until my death.

Babu Maraj leads puja on the banks of the Ganges River, Varanasi

That night I awoke soaked in cold sweat. I read the digital readout of my plastic five dollar wristwatch: 5:16 a.m. It felt as if I had slept only a few minutes, but I had actuall slumbered more than nine hours. Looking out the balcony window to the river below, I spied a family of five reverently holding a small white bundle as they boarded a water-logged rowboat. They struggled to the middle of the great river and placed the pristine package into the swift current. The water carried the carefully wrapped, immaculate bundle down stream.

Within minutes it had vanished from sight. The party quickly returned to shore and docked the boat directly below my window. The four men removed their clothing and bathed in the ink-black shallows of the Ganges.

Dressing again, they replaced their fine white clothing with ordinary street attire. As the first light of dawn crept over a bank of low clouds sitting on the horizon, the lone woman, still wearing her fine white linen dress, entered the chilly morning water and cleansed her soul of a tragic memory.

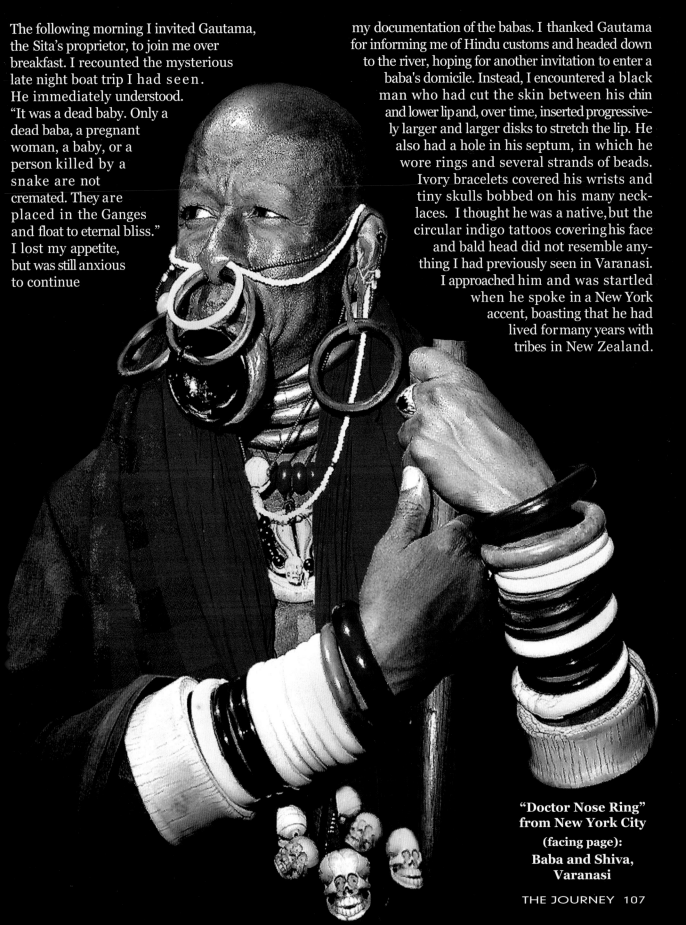

The following morning I invited Gautama, the Sita's proprietor, to join me over breakfast. I recounted the mysterious late night boat trip I had seen. He immediately understood. "It was a dead baby. Only a dead baba, a pregnant woman, a baby, or a person killed by a snake are not cremated. They are placed in the Ganges and float to eternal bliss." I lost my appetite, but was still anxious to continue my documentation of the babas. I thanked Gautama for informing me of Hindu customs and headed down to the river, hoping for another invitation to enter a baba's domicile. Instead, I encountered a black man who had cut the skin between his chin and lower lip and, over time, inserted progressively larger and larger disks to stretch the lip. He also had a hole in his septum, in which he wore rings and several strands of beads. Ivory bracelets covered his wrists and tiny skulls bobbed on his many necklaces. I thought he was a native, but the circular indigo tattoos covering his face and bald head did not resemble anything I had previously seen in Varanasi. I approached him and was startled when he spoke in a New York accent, boasting that he had lived for many years with tribes in New Zealand.

**"Doctor Nose Ring"
from New York City**

**(facing page):
Baba and Shiva,
Varanasi**

A naga sadhu wearing only a feathered hat and dozens of necklaces sat playing music on the river banks

I immediately lost interest in him and his ridiculous collection of nose rings when he explained he was from New York City and not from a primitive tribe. Wanting to get away; I told him I was in India surveying the babas and sadhus, and was now leaving to continue the documentary. He followed me and asked: "Do you know of the aghori babas?" "The aghori?" I anxiously inquired. "Yes, the aghori holy men eat and drink from human skulls! In trance they eat feces and flesh from cremated corpses, and drink urine. They live in huts with roofs made from clothing of the dead; their only other possession, other than the human skull they eat and drink from, is a whistle." I was skeptical, but later discovered everything he said was true. I left wondering what the blue-blooded, button-down, tassel-loafered ivy league set would think of him if he ever returned

A deformed nude midget baba, and hundreds of other holy men, set up tents on the banks of the Ganges

to his home in New York. I continued the sadhu search downstream, where I found an enormous influx of nomadic babas had set up tents in two rows on the east side of the Ganges since the previous time I had come that far downriver. As I passed through the forest of tents, salutations resounded, and invitations emanated, from deep within the countless lean-tos. Campfire soot and choking black vapor from the babas' hash hookahs mingled in the wind with white ash and blue smoke from cremation fires. I thought I was imagining hearing bells ring, but the further I went, the louder the sounds became. I soon encountered an unusual musical ensemble. Speaking in hushed tones, a deformed nude midget baba and a sadhu wearing only a feathered hat and dozens of necklaces sat playing enormous wooden drums while three other men rang six large bells.

Wearing elaborate hats with brass snake insignias, jangama sadhus ring bells for Shiva. Jangamas bless a copper lingam, a symbol of Shiva, on the banks of the Ganges; various musicians accompany the jangamas

The bell-ringing babas wore enormous helmets featuring black feathers, cobra insignias, and circular brass plates. They allowed me to join in the drum chorus, but only during the rhythm's bridge. "Who are those bell ringers with the big hats?" I asked the deformed nude midget baba after the three bell-playing

sadhus passed the hat and disappeared into the crowd. He did not speak English, but understood. "Jangama" was his only reply. I looked over at the white-painted face of the sadhu wearing the bead necklaces and asked, "Do you know about the jangamas?" "Yay, dee' are Shiva's minstrels," he replied in a heavy Hindi accent. "Dee' travel and stee' together, day' ring dee' bells for Lord Shiva. Da' is deer' destiny." A light blue cloud of smoke drifted above our heads as the nude midget passed around a hash-stuffed ceramic chillum with a wet cloth covering the mouthpiece. I discovered smoking hashish in public is socially acceptable behavior in India for sadhus and their guests, as two local policemen, armed with batons, patiently observed our consumption without interference.

I felt safe smelling the intoxicating aroma of opium-laced hash in the air as I gradually drifted into unconsciousness in the midget's tent. Hours later I awoke confused, disoriented and covered in ash blown down from the cremation fires upriver. My hands were blackened, my nostrils clogged, and the deformed midget baba was nowhere to be found.

Holy men smoke opium-laced hashish in chillums with sadhus hanging from trees and babas encircled in flaming cow dung

Hanging male and female sadhus, a baba encircled in burning cow dung, and two girls in the Ganges surrounded by buffalos.

I had trouble standing up, but was able to peer out from a hole in the tent, over two parallel rows of blue plastic and bamboo lean-tos, to a vacant lot where I could see a sadhu seated in the center of a circle of smoking cow dung. I went out and cautiously approached him. The odor caused me to sneeze violently, and the noise brought the sadhu out of his trace. But he quickly regained his composure. As a western wind off the Ganges fanned the flames of the smoking dung, his eyes rolled and he slipped back into oblivion.

Two other babas in the same lot hung on swings from a large tree, one male and the other a rare female sadhu. A soft, almost inaudible voice seemed to emanate through the hanging man rather than from him: "It is his penitence!" The eerie intonation made me retreat, but when he continued I was drawn back to his side as he explained. "Each day his guru tells him how many hours he must sit in a circle of burning dung. His full penitence is eighteen years, and in the final days of his sacrifice he must put a clay pot full of smoking dung cakes on his head."

Most of the holy men lived in plastic and bamboo lean-tos on the banks of the Ganges River

I questioned the hanging baba with the unearthly voice: "What about you? Why are you sitting in those swings?" His reply was almost as unbelievable as his explanation for the baba sitting in the circle of burning dung. "We will not sit down for twelve years. These swings keep us up. We have been standing now for more than seven years. We will stand for another five years, and then we will sit. This is our sacrifice to God." I wondered if they sat down when no one was looking, but eventually concluded that there are babas who have not sat down for more than twelve years, and others who sit in circles of burning excrement

Thousands of nomadic babas roam the streets of Varanasi

for even longer. Then and there I decided the experience I was having with the babas was getting to me. I needed to get away from it all, even if only for a short time. I thought a side trip might clear my head before I resumed my investigation of ascetic eccentricities. On several occasions over breakfast in the Sita's roof top restaurant, I had heard seasoned travelers discuss the merits of the Ramnagar Palace. Leaving the burning dung cakes to their own devices, I impulsively ran from the vacant lot and jumped into a dilapidated rickshaw that was heading down a back alley.

Ramnagar Palace contained antique auto
mobiles, costumes, weapons and roya
memorabilia from a lost era. The bare-bull
lighting and deteriorating facades wer
disappointing.

As the sun set, I hitched a ride back to the Sita by boat and met a bald Buddhist monk in radiant orange robes. He introduced himself as Shushat from Sarnarth. I asked about his home and he replied,

Sarnath

"Sarnath is where Lord Buddha first delivered his sermons, more than two thousand years ago. Sarnath is the most sacred Buddhist site in all of India. It is less than fifteen kilometers from here and can be easily reached in less than an hour." Shushat encouraged me to go there,

but said I would have to do so without him because he was leaving the next day on a two-day overland trip to Swayambhunath, the most sacred Buddhist temple in Nepal. Before the old monk politely dismissed me, I vowed to catch up with him!

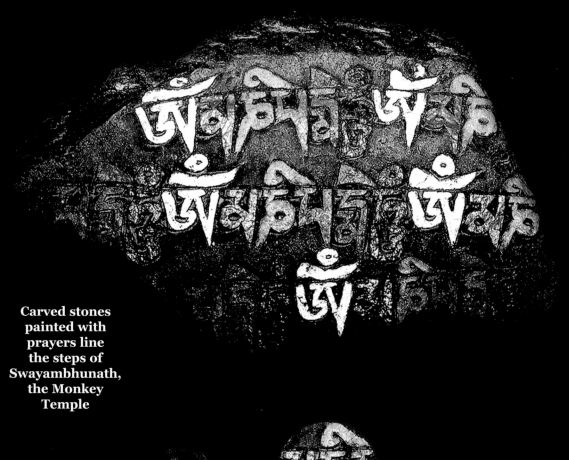

Carved stones
painted with
prayers line
the steps of
Swayambhunath,
the Monkey
Temple

The image of the old monk repeatedly flickered in my mind. I had promised to follow him, but why? My prudent side protested what I could not rationally explain; still, without even checking the bus schedule, I stuffed my camera equipment and filthy laundry into my backpack, checked out of the Sita, and took the first taxi I found to Varanasi's central depot. It took more than two full days of dusty travel on a variety of broken down, nearly treadless vehicles to arrive in Nepal's capital, Kathmandu, but when I caught sight of the "Monkey Temple," as the locals refer to Swayambhunath, I knew it had been worth it.

I had to sidestep seven cows and hordes of travelers to reach the recommended Kathmandu Peace Guest House. The proprietor, Raj, scrutinized my Nepali visa before welcoming me inside and showing me a room. There, he opened a terrace door and dramatically pointed to the Monkey Temple's majestic stupa towering in the distance over the elevated Buddhist enclave. "I'll take the room, thank you, Raj," I said. I had intended to find Sushat immediately at Swayambhunath, but exhaustion won out and I fell asleep fully dressed with my backpack still strapped over my shoulders. The next morning I awoke with Raj standing over me holding an overflowing tray of fruits, baked goods, nuts, and a large pot of black tea with a tiny serving of honey. Famished, I graciously accepted the offering, then left in search of the Monkey Temple and

**Shushat
the Buddhist monk**

(facing page):

**Novice monk at
Swayambhunath,
Kathmandu**

the wisdom of Swayambhunath's monastic inhabitants. A bouncing, black, canvas-covered, three-wheeled motor-cycle brought me from the guesthouse to the temple. It had a tiny meter, and, with rotating numer-als, it calculated the fare in Nepali rupees.

After exiting the exhaust-filled rear compartment, I began the arduous climb up the countless stairs to the Monkey Temple. Colorful Buddhist prayers were carved on boulders and stones lining the steps to the summit.

When I finally reached the entrance to Swayambhunath, a novice monk, in flowing red and orange robes, pros-trated himself before me and exclaimed, "Namaste." I did the same, realizing it must be a form of salutation. Later I learned that namaste is the most common Nepali greeting, meaning, "I bow to you." I said to the boy: "Shushat?"

went from his eyes into mine. The steady glow of the streaming spectrum lasted only moments, but after it subsided an inner peace took possession of my mind and body. "Like the yin and the yang," Shushat said, "you and I are one. As night and day can not be separated, you and I cannot be pulled apart. You know the ways of the world and I know the ways of the spirit. What you know I do not, and what I know you must learn. That is why you have come. I know you saw the light from my eyes go into yours."

A broad smile crossed his face and he led me down a circular stone staircase into the belly of the most sacred sanctum of Buddhism in Nepal. Before we reached our destination I detected a the beat of a single drum rhythmically repeated, accompanied by dirgelike chanting.progress. A ritual was in A few priests periodically blew conch shells in unison, accenting the trumpeting of thin horns. Far from me, close to the end of a line of monks, was Shushat. He indicated that he saw me by bowing his head slightly forward while opening and closing his eyes in time to the pulsating drum beat. The ritual concluded with a long series of call and response chants that blended with the sound of brass gongs struck with white silk-covered wooden mallets. After the ritual was over, Shushat spoke with me. "You traveled a great distance to meet me," he said. "I am impressed." His pupils dilated and a brilliant white light

Swayambhunath,
the Monkey Temple,
Kathmandu

(facing page):
Monks
at Swayambhunath

Monkeys flourish in great
numbers on the
temple grounds

For the duration of my stay I regularly dropped by the temple. Shushat instructed me in meditation and the use of mantras. He taught me how to slow my heartrate down to fifty beats per minute and to change my brain's electrical impulses from alpha to beta waves at will. In exchange I translated letters written in English and helped carry heavy loads up the endless stairways to the mountain-top retreat. I always feel a little culpable when I look back on my relationship with that old monk. He asked so little in return for the magnificent spiritual gifts he imparted.

Even though he and I were individual pieces that became one, I have never shaken the guilty feeling. My contribution to our relationship was so much smaller than his.

**Kathmandu
Nepal**

Kathmandu is an ancient city with a byzantine
network of twisting, turning, one-way passageways,
making it inhospitible to modern traffic and western-style
business. The narrow streets follow no coherent pattern and
allow only a single car to pass in any one direction at a
given time. Vehicles approaching from opposite directions
must stop, back up, and make way.

In the morning, of my fourth day in Kathmandu, I rented a bicycle. I aimlessly peddled through the city's tangled passageways until, on a tapered turn in a curved alley, an oncoming pack of rickshaws stopped my progress. My face was forced within inches of the wall of the Ring Road, which encircles Kathmandu. After the human-drawn carriages rolled past, I was able to back away from the wall, but before I resumed my ride, a poster written in English and glued to the wall caught my attention. I struggled to focus on the oversized full color notice that proudly stated, in bold lettering, "Bouddhanath a world heritage site."

Posters on the Ring Road wall, Kathmandu

On my next visit to the Monkey Temple I asked Shushat about Bouddhanath. "Yes, I have been there," he said. "It's not far. Only about five kilometers away. Tibetans love and honor Bouddhanath, believing it is the most important Buddhist temple in all of Nepal. This Monkey Temple is loved by Nepalis, but Bouddhanath is loved by Tibetans. Some walk all the way from Tibet to Nepal, just to go to Bouddhanath, and then they pray, crawling on their hands and knees in a circle all around the temple. From sunup to sundown they go around, around, and around." Five kilometers, only about a half-hour away. I was so excited I ran from the Monkey Temple into the street. In my haste, I stumbled over a vendor's cart.

I almost smashed the glass element in my camera as I fell, but at the last instant the vendor pushed his rolling display out of the way and saved me from an even more unpleasant experience. I hailed another black, canvas-covered, three-wheeled taxi, which dropped me at Bouddhanath.

The temple turned out to be even more exotic than I had anticipated. It is so old that history failed to record who built it, though myths and folktales trace its origin back to the fifth century. The events that actually spurred Bouddhanath's growth may never come to light, but the Buddhist traditions that germinated the temple and caused it to flourish are still intact.

A lamp perpetually burns in Bouddhanath. No one knows when the lamp was first lit, but if it were ever accidentally extinguished, it could only be re-lit by a flame brought from the old Monkey Temple at Swayambhunath.

Bouddhanath Temple

Tibetan woman

Mandala painting

One of the
eight corners of
Bhaktapur,
protected by
a Hindu
goddess statue

The next morning a soft voice drew my consciousness from a deep sleep. "Dave, are you up? Dave, can you hear me? Are you awake?" I was tempted to say "Dave's not here!" but knew it would only be confusing, so I cracked the door open a few inches. Raj, the guest house proprietor, poked his nose in and said: "Somebody's here ta' see ya." After I threw on some shorts he escorted me into the dank northern side of the guest house's mildewing restaurant. A stranger dressed in a red and white Tommy Hilfiger T-shirt sat patiently

waiting. I knew I was about to be hustled. "Good morning! They call me Keshab! Raj tells me you are touring Kathmandu. I can show you many, many, things you have not seen. If you like, I can guide you!" I pumped him for useful information. His brief portrayal of a city called Bhaktapur was enticing. "Bhaktapur," he said, "has been protected for a thousand years by eight female Hindu goddess statues, one at each corner of the city."

(above): Earthenware drying in the sun

Keshab and I went to the stairway of a fourteenth-century temple in the heart of Bhaktapur's Durbar Square and began to climb. When we had nearly reached the top I found a disappointing handwritten notice on a scrap of wood: "HINDUS ONLY. NO ENTRY." "Do you hear music?" I asked Keshab. "I'm not sure. I go scout, come back, and tell you. Do ya' want me to go see?" he questioned in his singsong voice. "OK," I said. "Go ahead, but if you get lost or don't come right back, our deal is off and I pay you nothing. Agreed?" With a nod he sheepishly consented. I continued the slow ascent to the highest landing of the temple. From there I could see what Keshab had gone to investigate.

here was a procession moving from the outskirts of Bhaktapur toward Durbar Square. Keshab raced back, bellowing, "It's a birthday!" Attempting to control a bout of giddy laughter, he blurted out "They carry an old man on a throne! Four bearers! And his wife! Beautiful young virgins dressed in their finest, and many people follow, play music. You wanna see?" Keshab's passionate assessment actually underrated the ostentatious opulence of the gala and the extent of the its drama. Earsplitting music merged with color as the congregation of adorned virgins assembled within view. The golden threads in their gowns shimmered violently in the noonday sun, initiating a sensory overload as my reality melted into a dream.

Virgin goddesses at a birthday celebration in Bhaktapur's Durbar Square

Cognition briefly resumed only long enough for me to hear the crowds cheering chorus. "He's seventy years old today... It's a very special day... For all of us today... He's seventy years old today!" As the circular chant continued, its incessant refrain called me back to incoherent hallucinations.

As I drifted in and out of reality, the frantic, undulating crowd kept pulling Keshab further and further away from me until I finally lost him.

A birthday party for a seventy-year-old man on the streets of Bhaktapur

Beautifully-colored sounds blended with extraordinary-smelling colors. An ocean of consolidated sight and sound engulfed me and dragged me into the festivities of the advancing mob. At dusk rain began to fall, forcing an end to my frenzy. As refreshing raindrops spattered my face I slowly revived, awakening from a delirious abstraction that I cannot clearly remember but will never forget.

Kumari, virgin goddesses

(facing page): A Hindu priest, shrines, and festivals

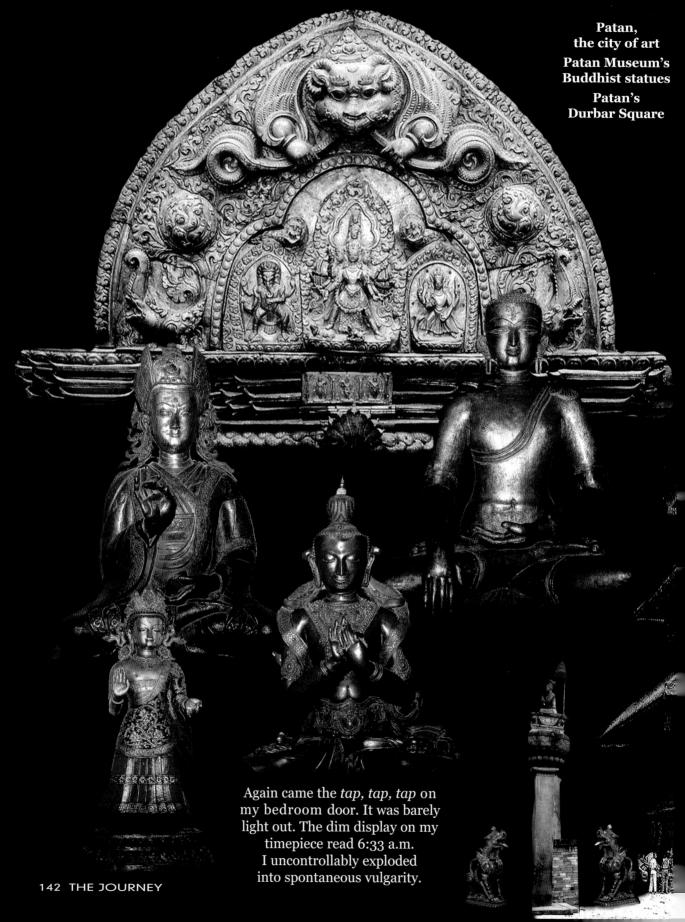

**Patan,
the city of art**

**Patan Museum's
Buddhist statues**

**Patan's
Durbar Square**

Again came the *tap, tap, tap* on
my bedroom door. It was barely
light out. The dim display on my
timepiece read 6:33 a.m.
I uncontrollably exploded
into spontaneous vulgarity.

I thought about driving the intruder from my door, but curiosity got the best of me. I bounded out of bed, energized and hoping for more of Keshab's unpredictable adventures. Wrapped in a mosquito net, I opened the portal. It was Keshab. I apologized for my rude outburst. "You wanna go ta' Patan?" he asked. "Yes," I replied. "You talked about it yesterday, but I can't remember what you said!"

Patan is a magical, ancient enclave, overflowing with primeval nooks and crannies and crammed with time-worn artifacts and architecture. Behind an elaborately-detailed gilded door facing a beautifully decorated courtyard, archaic royal palaces hold some of the finest works of Asian art in the world. I began photographing a mammoth cantilevered brass bell over the main entrance to Patan, but was hindered by vendors constantly underfoot hawking their wares. "You want to stop bullets? You want to stop H.I.V.? Stop H.I.V.? Stop bullets," a very young girl sirened while holding a small brass figure of a dragon in her right hand and a glass vial containing dark sepia colored liquid in her left. "Flying metal and an invincible virus can not be stopped by your statues and liquids," I snapped. "I'm sure you understand that, don't you?" "Yes they can!" she insisted. "You see dragon? The one who holds this can never be shot." She handed me the small metal figurine for examination. It was four or five inches tall. Its front right foot had partially broken off, and it looked as if it had once been

attached to a base. After digging through her purse she proudly presented what had once been a full eight-and-a-half by eleven piece of paper. The document appeared to represent some kind of assessment or formal appraisal. She read it aloud with great fervor, in a tone normally reserved for politicians. "The Highest Court of the Land, and Anthropological

A child vendor sold H.I.V. cures and a dragon statue that stopped bullets

(this and facing page):
Plastic bags full of curative herbs
Patan's bell

and Archeological divisions of State and Cultural Affairs Departments, value this artifact in excess of 2,000,000 rupees."

"This dragon stops nothing! I don't care what your paper says," I screamed in rage, demanding to know where she had gotten the abominable piece of junk and the fraudulent paper-work. I requested a revolver for proof, but she declined, basing her response on the fact that in Nepal possession of firearms is illegal. After a lengthy interview I finally decided the child truly believed the inanimate brass toy miraculously prevented injury from gunfire. I considered inquiring about the item she purported would cure H.I.V., but after thinking for only a moment, I decided to silently slip away.

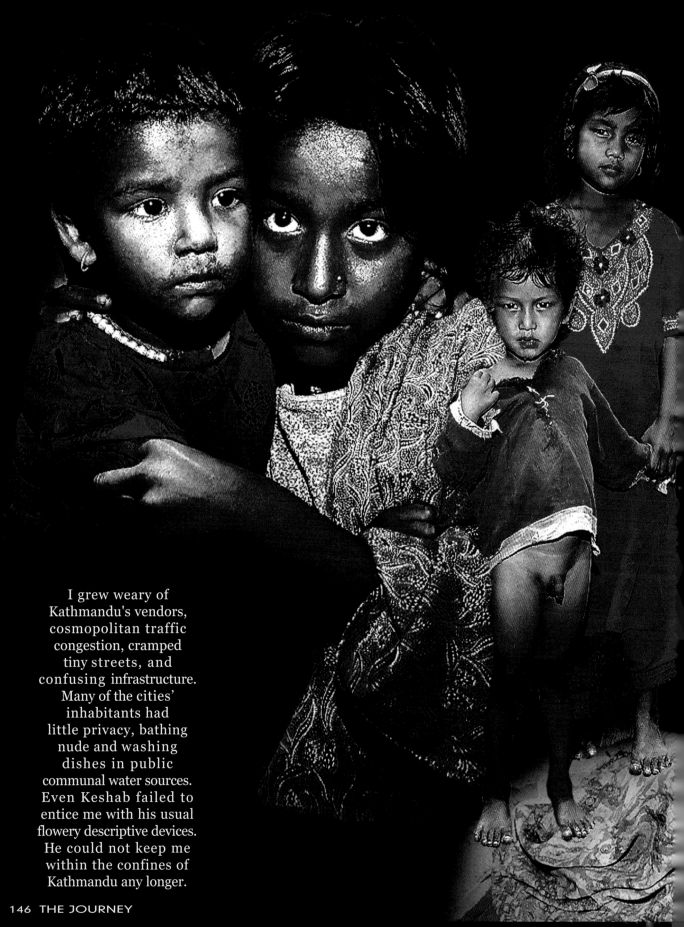

I grew weary of
Kathmandu's vendors,
cosmopolitan traffic
congestion, cramped
tiny streets, and
confusing infrastructure.
Many of the cities'
inhabitants had
little privacy, bathing
nude and washing
dishes in public
communal water sources.
Even Keshab failed to
entice me with his usual
flowery descriptive devices.
He could not keep me
within the confines of
Kathmandu any longer.

I still wanted to explore the inner city, but I needed a break. I just had to get out. I decided the easiest way was to wander on foot to the edge of the city. I was not certain were I was headed, but the further I got from the center of Kathmandu the better I felt. Walking west, I passed over the Vishnumati River, then crossed the Ring Road. When I had gotten that far, I felt completely rejuvenated. Distant mountains appeared close enough to reach and return from before dark. The one-lane blacktop cluttered with rickshaws, bicycles, motorcycles, and tiny vans eventually petered out into a dirt road that gracefully careened over gently-sloping tree-topped hills.

Families publically bathe on the streets in communal water sources, Kathmandu

The further I walked the more rural it became, until Kathmandu's traffic noise was replaced by welcoming greetings from farm children. I was astonished, after strolling only two or three hours, to find rolling cornfields and modest, free-standing farm houses surrounded by acres of open land. A pack of smiling kids guided me to their parents harvesting food in the fields, but my presence put a strain on their daily routine. Because I was a stranger they refused all overtures and stopped me from taking their portraits. Only one old man knew any English at all, and the only thing he said was: "Evil eye.... Evil eye.... Evil eye!" I had to disarm the threat instilled by the old folk tale that a camera captures and steals the spirit of its subject.

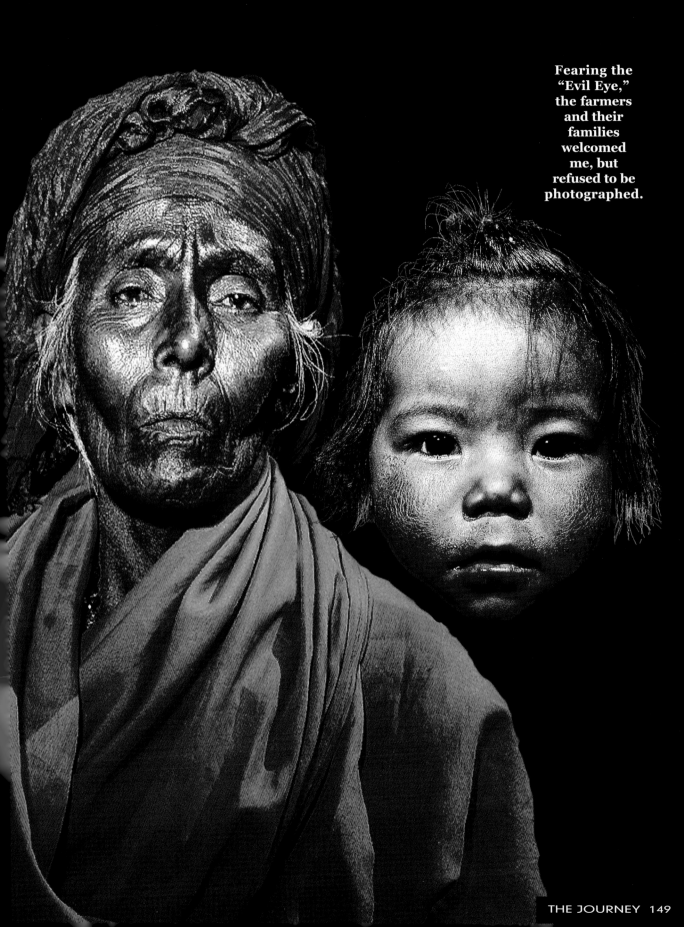

Fearing the "Evil Eye," the farmers and their families welcomed me, but refused to be photographed.

I devised a crude
but original form
of communication
that eventually won
the farmer's hearts
and minds:
I mimicked the
sound of laughter
every time I wanted
to take their picture.
That did the trick.
I intoned the
nonsensical
exclamation
"Hee … hee!"
It was persuasive.
I uttered the
silly salutation
at every available
opportunity, and
after hearing the
repetitious ring
of my childlike
mock mirth over
and over and
over again, they
accepted me and
allowed me to
take their pictures.

By then the sun was setting and the moon rising, which left little or no light for photography. As fireplaces dimly illuminated the inside of the farmers' homes, I could see one family, sitting in a circle around a blaze, beginning to eat their dinner. "Come in! Eat, eat, eat, eat! I will not accept no for an answer," the patriarch of the house cried. He was so forceful that I questioned his motives as I hesitantly consented to the offer and cautiously entered his domain.

A farmer's wife and baby

(facing page): **The farmer who invited me to dinner**

"Don't you understand?" the old farmer wailed. "Your sight taints our food and my loved ones will become very sick if they eat it! We Nepalis strongly believe if we do not give you some, after you see our meal, my whole family will suffer severe and dire consequences." From then on I let down my guard. As he served the food he explained that it would become "jutho," contaminated, if I served myself. It was also considered humiliating if I gave any of my food or drink portions to anyone else in the family. I noticed he offered bits from his plate to his wife and children. By then, constant outbursts of uncontrollable laughter, punctuated with uncovered yawns, slowly faded in the twilight of

the evening's cloud-covered full moon and the hearth's dying embers. My failing eyesight strained to make out the time on a wall-mounted, battery-powered Mickey Mouse clock. "What's the time?" From out of the darkness, a faceless family member turned on a tiny Maglight and pointed it at the rodent timepiece. I now could clearly see Mickey's right hand on the 10 and his left on the 20. The family's matriarch whispered in monotone less than an inch from my left ear: "Please, you should stay. It is too late. Stay here with us, please?" I knew it would be a fool's errand, potentially filled with more uncomfortable consequences, if I set out now in an attempt to reach Kathmandu in the dark.

Rural families
harvesting corn

Half the family already slumbered around the fireplace in one big bundle. If another person joined them, they would not notice, and the ones still awake did not seem to care.

I reluctantly responded, "Thank you. You are very kind. It is too late to try and get back. I will sleep with you and your family. Thank you. Thank you so much."

I slept very peacefully after accepting the fact that I was stranded. In the morning I was the first to awake. My stirring disturbed the patriarch, who quickly rose and followed me into the pre-dawn darkness. We did not speak. I left with only a handshake. When I crossed the furthest hilltop, still in sight of his home, pink and orange sunlight creased the bottom of the dawn's low-lying fog,

The family who gave me supper and a place to sleep when I was stranded.

and as I looked back from this last possible vantage point, I surveyed his farm a final time. I could see him, standing motionless with his wife, as if they were guardian angels making sure I was safely on my journey. I had reluctantly stayed the night, but now, with even greater regret, I disappeared forever from their sight.

Tap, tap, tap ... tap, tap, tap ... It was that wood-pecker again, tapping, tapping, tapping on my bedroom door. Exhausted from the trek to the farmlands, I thought about not responding, but knowing my time in Kathmandu would soon come to an end, I did not want to miss an opportunity to explore places within the city I might have overlooked. "Yes, who is it?" "It's me, Raj. Keshab is downstairs and he wants to know if you want to go to Pashupatinath."

Keshab and I took a rick-shaw this time. I felt sorry for the boy who pedaled the contraption. He made the job look easy, but by the time we got to Pashupatinath, a temple site in Kathmandu and the most important cremation area in Nepal, he was drenched in sweat. As Keshab and I entered, we were sucked into a spiritual sideshow of holy men, monkeys, five-legged sacred cows, hash salesman and public toilets with no running water.

Pashupatinath, Nepal
Cremation fires
Rickshaw driver
Five-legged cow
Holy men and monkeys
Namisga, the death ritual

After we squeezed though the crowded entrance, Keshab guided me to the ghats, the cremation platforms suspended over the Bagmati River. Groups of shaven-headed men, clad only in white, clustered by the bridge. Keshab explained, "Following the death of a loved one, family members participate in namisga for thirteen days."

Keshab went on to describe katto, the namisga death ritual's eleventh day after cremation. "Katto ensures the deceased will find peace. The rite requires a brahmin's sacrifice, a holy man who takes on the burden of the dead person's soul by eating an unclean meal. The brahmin, riding an elephant, is then expelled from Kathmandu Valley. If a woman runs between the legs of the elephant, it is foretold she will conceive a son, perhaps the reincarnation of the deceased person." As we crossed the Bagmati River, dense blue cremation smoke from fires north and south of the bridge engulfed us. Corpses smeared in several pounds of butter to insure complete incineration crackled in the flames. I could smell and hear the sizzling flesh cook, as an approaching monsoon's raindrops hissed on contact with the fires.

Ritually annointed
male corpse prepared
for cremation

Flower garlands, beads,
and colored powder

(facing page):
Cremation sequence

As I photographed one of the cadavers being consumed in flames, I was approached by a distraught family member aggressively wailing, "Why, why, why do you take pictures of my dead brother?"

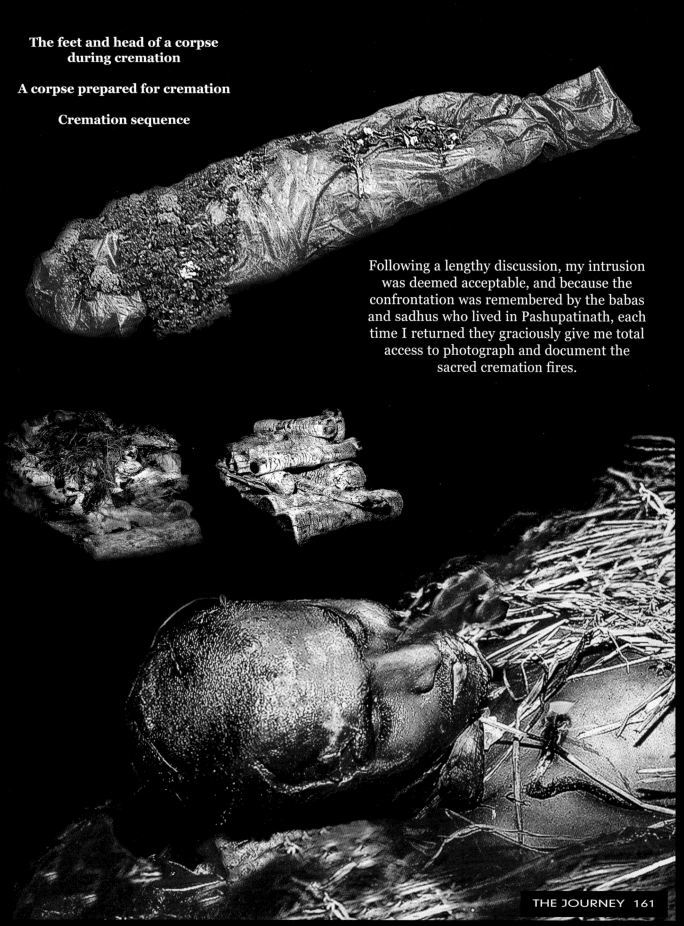

The feet and head of a corpse during cremation

A corpse prepared for cremation

Cremation sequence

Following a lengthy discussion, my intrusion was deemed acceptable, and because the confrontation was remembered by the babas and sadhus who lived in Pashupatinath, each time I returned they graciously give me total access to photograph and document the sacred cremation fires.

Four corpses ready for cremation; temples, Pashupatinath, Kathmandu

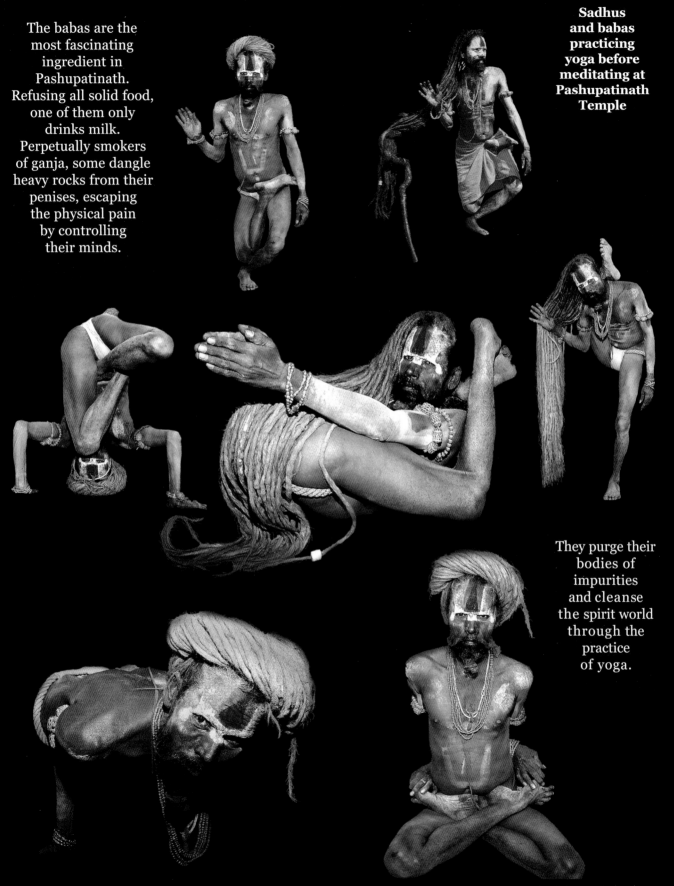

The babas are the most fascinating ingredient in Pashupatinath. Refusing all solid food, one of them only drinks milk. Perpetually smokers of ganja, some dangle heavy rocks from their penises, escaping the physical pain by controlling their minds.

Sadhus and babas practicing yoga before meditating at Pashupatinath Temple

They purge their bodies of impurities and cleanse the spirit world through the practice of yoga.

Babas in a Pashupatinath courtyard waiting for a samashti feast

After we escaped the smoke of the cremation fires, Keshab and I crossed the Bagmati River and entered the babas' compound through one of Pashupatinath's many ancient arched stone doorways. There we found hundreds of holy men seated on the cement floor in the courtyard. Keshab presumed the babas would soon enjoy a samashti feast, a banquet donated by wealthy Hindus who hope to have their wealth blessed by the holy men. Eventually meals were brought out and placed in front of each one. Some greedily devoured the offering, but most drifted off, refusing to eat, while others transcended reality, escaping into trance. Over my left shoulder, from within a room behind a half-open door, I could faintly hear the sound of young voices. "Are you coming to Pashupatinath for Shivaratri?" I ventured closer to the threshold hoping to hear more. "The Milk Baba will be there, and all who honor Shiva. When is it?" "The big day is next week, Wednesday, the twenty-first, but there are events the day before the

festival and the day after." It was February, and from what I could gather from their banter, a spectacular Pashupatinath event was to take place in less than a week. I felt guilty eavesdropping on their conversation but could no longer contain myself. I had to confront them. "I can hear you talking about Shivaratri," I said, pushing the door completely open. "I just came from India, and don't know anything about Pashupatinath or Shivaratri. Can you tell me about them?" The pair were covered from head to foot in wet whitewash. They were brushing the cream-colored paint on the interior walls of a baba's bedroom, while a black and white television featuring a Nepali drama lit the room.

More eager than patient, the boys attempted to satisfy their own curiosity. "We can tell ya' what ya' wanna
know, but from what country da' ya' come from?" After revealing my place of origin I responded to their
ceaseless inquisition by repeating my original query: "Please explain to me, what is Shivaratri?"
Before receiving my answer I had to satisfy the pair by fielding an endless rock and roll quiz.
One finally said: "Oh yah' I can tell ya'. Shivaratri is our annual gathering of babas. They come from
all over India and Nepal to meet at Pashupatinath. Everyone can smoke charas that day. No police

Babas and
sadhus from all
across India and
Nepal come to
Pashupatinath
once a year
to celebrate
Shivaratri

problems. The festival goes on all day and all night. It's a really big party!" The one covered in the most paint gracefully picked up where the other had left off without skipping a beat. "And even though Pashupatinath is Lord Shiva's home on earth, we still build thousands of bonfires to keep him warm in the place he lives way up high above in the sky." I had difficulty restraining my enthusiasm during the five days prior to Shivaratri. Pacing the floor of the Kathmandu Peace Guesthouse, I wondered how my imagination of the event would compare with the reality of the experience.

Every day before Shivaratri I returned to Pashupatinath to document the fires, survey the site, and scout out the best possible locations for the festival. Tossing and turning with anticipation, I could barely sleep the night before. I dressed by candlelight. When dawn finally broke, the dim yellow patches of sun that fell on my bleached white bed sheets became the only illumination as my candle died in a flicker of smoke. I was so geared up it was impossible to eat while I silently drank cold black tea in a damp, windowless restaurant. When I arrived at the festival

Nepali babas at Pashupatinath's Shivaratri Festival, Kathmandu

there were so many people
it took more than three
hours of thrusting through
the throngs of boisterous
revelers before I reached
the babas' compound on
the east side of
Pashupatinath's stone
bridge. There I found a
surreal atmosphere that
forever shattered my
cultural notions
concerning behavior.
A milling mob of
totally nude sadhus
paraded single file,
counterclockwise,
in a circle, chanting.
Powdered from
head to foot in pale
blue ash from incinerated
human bodies, they
passed chillums and
hookahs stuffed with
smoldering hashish
from hand to hand.

Bamboo poles, sword blades, broomsticks, metal rods and other handy objects were wrapped around testicles and penises, which were then tied into knots. Some babas sat in circles of smoldering cow dung, oblivious to the outside world, so deep in meditative trance that even raindrops did not wake them.

Smoke from simmering bodies engulfed in cremation fires clouded the sky and blocked the sunlight. As it grew dark, the rib-crushing crowds grew larger. It took longer to exit from Pashupatinath than it did to enter. For several hours, in flickering light from unstable voltage, I tried to segregate myself from the crazed, seemingly inescapable, gelatinous mass of undulating humanity and struggled in vain to exit the temple.

Sadhus on the Bagmati River, Shivaratri Festival, Pashupatinath, Kathmandu

I squirmed through the crowd to a point where I could see the outer perimeter of the festival. I glimpsed traffic moving in and out of the event, but before I could reach the mobbed taxi stand within Pashupatinath, I ran into an enormous group of bearded Indian babas waiting in a food line.

I envisioned stepping down the line, baba by baba, taking individual and group portraits. I asked permission by holding my camera high above my head and saying the single word sentence: "Photo?"

My intent was undeniable, but the babas' response was definitely negative. I wanted pictures of those sadhus at all cost, so I pleaded with the first three in line.

I begged, and then tried bribery, offering twenty rupees to each for his cooperation. That changed everything. They snapped to attention and were even willing to take directions. After I had hopscotched from group to group, photographing some and skipping others, the babas I had passed over realized they were not going to be rewarded. As I approached the final cluster of sadhus I wanted to shoot,

the ever-expanding collection of rejected babas surrounded me. In lieu of receiving a monetary reward in exchange for their portraits, they now hoped to separate me from my money by offering a variety of items for sale.

Babas on the Bagmati River, Shivaratri Festival, Pashupatinath

Holy men, Shivaratri Festival, Pashupatinath

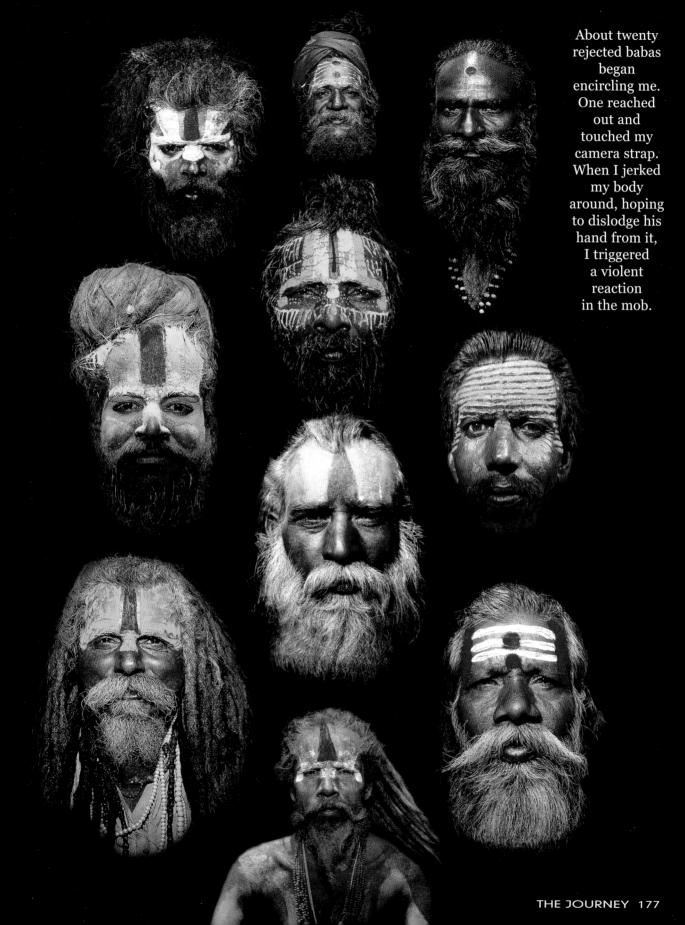

About twenty rejected babas began encircling me. One reached out and touched my camera strap. When I jerked my body around, hoping to dislodge his hand from it, I triggered a violent reaction in the mob.

The babas charged, and dozens of hands reached for the contents of my pockets. I hit the dirt and crawled quickly through the sadhus' legs on my hands and knees. The side pocket of my jacket and the back pockets of my pants were almost completely torn off, and remained only as dangling pieces of cloth. In a frantic race to Pashupatinath's taxi stand I outdistanced the babas, pushed people aside, jumped the line, and ran into the only available cab. Once the waiting passengers realized I was being pursued, they helped by slamming my door shut, then rushing in front of the cab to prevent any further assault. I screamed, "DRIVE!" The cabbie let out a blue cloud of burning tire rubber, his clutch grinding, in the wrong gear.

The Indian
babas who
ripped open
my pockets at
Shivaratri

A Himalayan sky
and a Nepali
porter

A girl in Jomosom

The dirt
landing field at
Jomosom's
airfield

The following morning I assessed the 1,232 photographs of holy men I had shot in India and Nepal. After deciding I had taken enough, I wondered: now that I have finished the sadhu survey, what will I do with the eight remaining days I have in Nepal before my departure? The violent experience with the holy men convinced me that the baba project was complete. The gods had been with me so far. Perhaps it would be unwise to push my luck. I played it safe and did not even venture out of the guest house, but I needed fresh air and wanted to be alone, so I climbed the spiral staircase to the roof. When I reached the top I found another loner deep in thought, sitting in a lotus position, reading a book. At first we ignored each other, but we slowly sensed we were cut from the same cloth. Looking up from a copy of *Into Thin Air,* he said, "I've just come back from a two month trek around Annapurna." He went on to describe sacred sanctuaries in the Himalayas in a tale that left me dumbfounded.

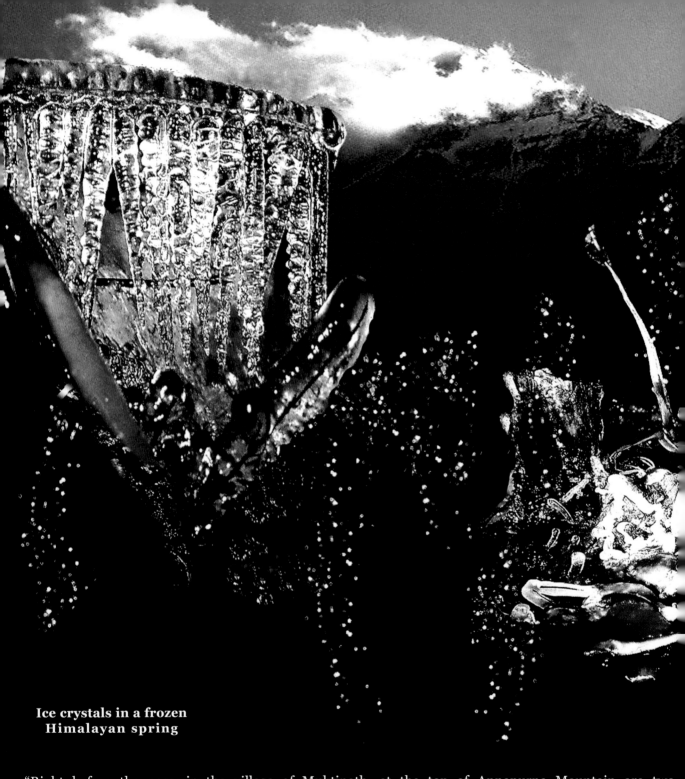

**Ice crystals in a frozen
Himalayan spring**

"Right before the pass, in the village of Muktinath, at the top of Annapurna Mountain are two temples where you can see water, air, fire and earth come together naturally." I silently questioned the description, and weighed the possibility of reaching the Himalayan mountain retreat. Had temples actually been built over natural burning gas jets submerged in spring water? I ran back to my room and began packing, determined to reach Muktinath. I checked out of the guesthouse and walked to Candi Pot, the bus terminal across from the Royal Palace. I boarded a bus and took a six hour ride to Pokhara. There I bought a ticket on the next available flight halfway up Annapurna to the tiny town

of Jomosom. The forty-five minute flight saved me a five-day uphill trek. The old 16-seater passenger plane gracefully traversed a virginal section of Himalayan mountains, but when it approached Jomosom I came to a frightening realization: Jomosom's landing strip was only made of dirt! The pilot confidently circled several times before negotiating a short, extraordinarily steep, descent between two mountain peaks. With precision he let the aircraft fall, engines off, onto the potholed, pockmarked airfield for a terrifying, almost out of control, touchdown. After getting off the plane I did not bother to stop and look at the three-block town. I just kept on walking.

Mule teams packing supplies upcountry through the Annapurna Pass

I kept telling myself, "It's simply a matter of following directions," each time I referred to a five- by seven-inch map of the area I was exploring. I had to get to the tiny outpost of Eklobhatti first; from there it would be an easy trek to the last destination of the day, Kagbeni. Trains of donkeys and mules bearing supplies steadily negotiated the narrow, rocky path. Making rapid progress was impossible. I approached one of the mule drivers while pointing in the direction of a dry river bed and asked, "Kagbeni?" Without a word he pointed down the parched river toward a canyon that disappeared between two imposing mountains.

The mule driver suggested the dry riverbed route through the Himalayan canyon

There was no path, but in the distance I could make out a pass between the peaks. The trail I was following snaked up and down the rugged, sloping terrain, parallel to the river bed. The map showed Kagbeni was on that path, but the mule driver's hand hung in the air indicating that his recommendation was down the dry riverbed and through the canyon. The only path I could make out was a twisting network of indistinct lines running up and along the barren slopes. The riverbed, on the other hand, was a straight shot running flat to the north. It did not take me long to decide to take a chance on the local shortcut.

The river ran through a canyon; on the mountain's face were caves

I hoped the man's directions would get me to Kagbeni before dark. However, there proved to be an unforeseen problem with the route. It forced me between running river water and a higher west bank. I had to crawl along precarious overhanging trails above the dwindling tributary, on extremely narrow hidden ledges, to pass over enormous river boulders. Constrained by a blind ascent, I anxiously searched for any chance to get to the river's east side. The grade of the trail steadily rose until it was necessary to climb up and onto the face of the mountain. But I swung around on the last free climb to the ridge I realized the directions I had received were excellent. A wood and wire suspension bridge hung over the gap between

Porters carry supplies up Annapurna en route to Kagbeni

the river's east and west banks across what seemed like a mile-high divide that separated me from Eklobhatti. Running across the bridge, I glanced at my watch and found there were less than two hours of daylight left. I looked up and saw the dim outline of the outpost. Eklobhatti turned out to be only a few buildings, not a town. The only sound there was the occasional *hee haw* of a donkey and the unforgiving echo of the Himalayan winds. I stayed only a few minutes. Anxiety triggered me to run until I set eyes on the shadowed path to Kagbeni. Within an hour I could see it on the horizon. As I entered the ancient Himalayan enclave I saw that it had survived for centuries almost unchanged.

A woman rests on the trail under a full moon

Mules packing supplies upcountry

The free climb to the river's east side

The riverbed route

Porters carrying wooden beams up the mountain

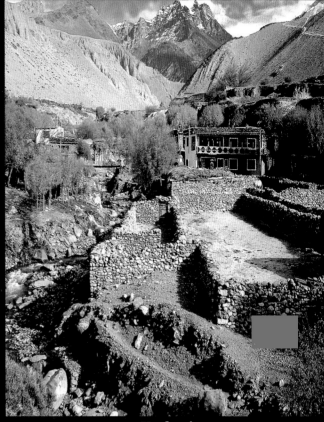
Kagbeni

Kagbeni, in a canyon on a river

Kagbeni

The next day, before dawn, I awoke at the Trekker's Lodge in Kagbeni with a splitting headache. At only 9200 feet above sea level, the altitude was already taking its toll. It was far too cold to venture out, so I went back to bed, where I enjoyed a breakfast of hot oatmeal and cold coffee. A few hours later it had warmed up enough to comfortably roam through Kagbeni. I discovered a trail of fresh blood on the cobblestone walkway that wove through the village. I followed the still-steaming crimson liquid to a closed door and knocked. As I opened the door and peered inside, a woman gasped. I turned to leave, but a man ushered me in as he exited. Inside the twelve-foot-high, stone-walled enclosure, I found a family soaked in blood encircling a yak carcass, which they were butchering. The strongest family members hacked through the ribcage with large machetes. Others used small axes to remove meat from the bones, and still others tossed the bloody entrails into a large basket.

I quickly lost interest in the activity, but a mother of three who had requested some of the less palatable remains won my attention after she accepted a gift of the animal's head and feet. I helped her carry the still-bleeding remains back to her home. No matter how hard we tried, we could not get the head through the old wooden doorway of her hut.

Priya and her children

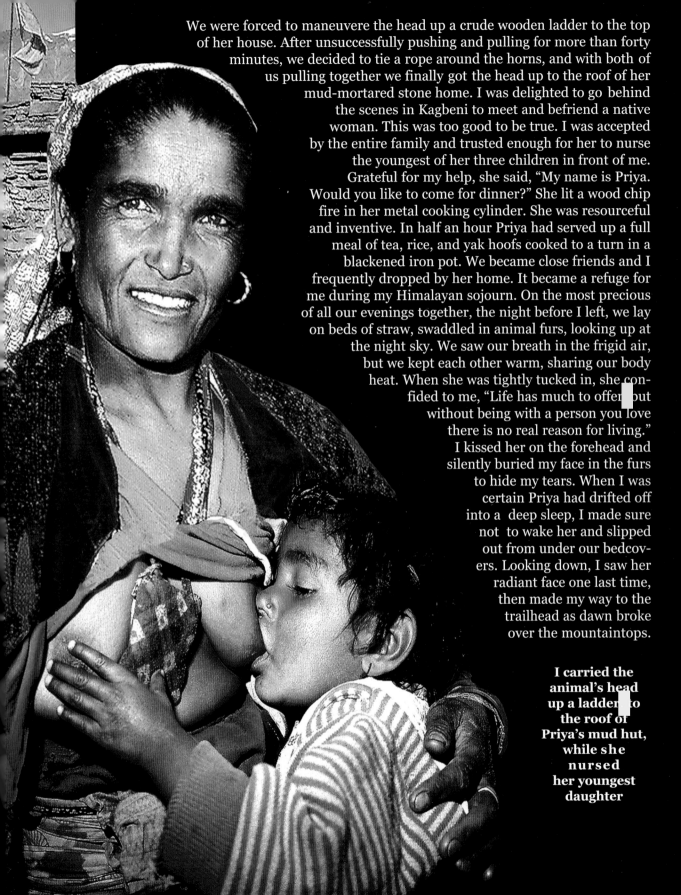

We were forced to maneuvere the head up a crude wooden ladder to the top of her house. After unsuccessfully pushing and pulling for more than forty minutes, we decided to tie a rope around the horns, and with both of us pulling together we finally got the head up to the roof of her mud-mortared stone home. I was delighted to go behind the scenes in Kagbeni to meet and befriend a native woman. This was too good to be true. I was accepted by the entire family and trusted enough for her to nurse the youngest of her three children in front of me. Grateful for my help, she said, "My name is Priya. Would you like to come for dinner?" She lit a wood chip fire in her metal cooking cylinder. She was resourceful and inventive. In half an hour Priya had served up a full meal of tea, rice, and yak hoofs cooked to a turn in a blackened iron pot. We became close friends and I frequently dropped by her home. It became a refuge for me during my Himalayan sojourn. On the most precious of all our evenings together, the night before I left, we lay on beds of straw, swaddled in animal furs, looking up at the night sky. We saw our breath in the frigid air, but we kept each other warm, sharing our body heat. When she was tightly tucked in, she confided to me, "Life has much to offer but without being with a person you love there is no real reason for living." I kissed her on the forehead and silently buried my face in the furs to hide my tears. When I was certain Priya had drifted off into a deep sleep, I made sure not to wake her and slipped out from under our bedcovers. Looking down, I saw her radiant face one last time, then made my way to the trailhead as dawn broke over the mountaintops.

I carried the animal's head up a ladder to the roof of Priya's mud hut, while she nursed her youngest daughter

The map I studied in the early morning light showed a steady uphill climb to Muktinath. At nearly 12,000 feet I would have to pass through the remote, isolated village of Jharkot. I wanted to avoid the possibility of a distressing emotional upheaval for Priya, so I quietly stole out of Kagbeni.

The isolated Himalayan outpost: "Jharkot"

Singlemindededly, I continued ascending. The air thinned as I advanced, making the climb progressively more difficult. Altitude sickness seemed inevitable, until I finally spied a mountaintop ruin miles in the distance. Hoping this was Jharkot, I picked up the pace, looking for shelter from the howling Himalayan wind.

Some of Jharkot's
inhabitants had not
washed or changed their
clothes in years

Jharkot was so primitive I felt I had stepped back a thousand years in time. Many of the buildings were made only of mud and stone. Exhausted from the mountain trek, I checked into the first tea house I stumbled over and awoke the next day refreshed and eager to explore the village.

A weaver and her three sisters offered me a variety of questionable food products after learning I had eaten insects

I wandered through Jharkot until I met a woman carrying a long bamboo pole. "What are you doing with that rod?" I inquired. She tersely replied, "I hunt for food!" Curiosity forced me to follow her to ferret out prey. I ended up helping poke and prod the bamboo pole, with a gummy paste applied to its tip, into natural and artificial cracks and crevices throughout the entire village for hours, until I finally realized she was hunting for bugs. I was famished by the time she had collected a variety of insects, and even though it was not my usual breakfast fare, I felt grateful for the unusual protein sustenance I normally would never have consider swallowing. In fact, I relished it. I continued meandering through Jharkot, feeling my exploration was somehow incomplete, when I happened upon a weaver, her three sisters, and a niece, all drinking tea. I told them about the insects I had just consumed. When they learned I was willing to eat the local food, they offered me various dishes of mysterious content, whose flavors I savored and devoured for lunch.

Buddhist pilgrims marked the way to Muktinath with painted stone stupas

I did not stay a full day in Jharkot. Muktinath was only a couple of hours up the mountain. I could see the Thorung La Pass through Annapurna's peaks at 18,000 feet, but reaching it was another matter. To steel my courage I pretended I was an ill-equipped Buddhist pilgrim I had recently met. Travelers have criss-crossed the Himalayas for thousands of years on foot, leaving piles of rocks for trail markers and building crude but colorful stupas as guideposts. I took my mind off the difficulty of the climb by imagining a glimpse of eternity burning in a pool of water. I remembered the strange promise of temples cradled on mountaintops, that reveal precious metaphysical secrets through their

Himalayan mountain trail markers guide worshippers to sacred sites

perpetual fires. Each encounter with a stone marker renewed my determination, as I fought off the fear that all my struggle might be in vain. Although the path was sometimes hard to see, I felt assured that the Vishnu and Iwalla Mai temples did in fact exist. I was eventually welcomed by the impressive, imposing gates to Mukinath. But still I continued having an uneasy feeling that my journey would be futile. In fact, I was trapped in a daydream. My mind repeatedly recycled the idea that I had forgotten certain important details which could have otherwise prevented me from getting lost and becoming stranded here forever.

I envisioned the temples lying in wait just on the other side of Muktinath's grand entry, but was disappointed when after passing through the gates I found only the same dirt path which led to Muktinath.

The Hindu Vishnu and
Buddhist Iwalla
Mai temples

Muktinath
is a mystical enclave in
the Himalayan Mountains

As the sun set I became anxious, and questioned the first
person I encountered. "Where are the temples?" "The temples?"
"Yes, the temples with the eternal burning fires. I was told Hindu and
Buddhist temples are in Muktinath and I have come a very long
way to pray here. Do you know of them?"

I asked two women, who wore matching paisley bandannas, turquoise necklaces, and green and red jackets, "Where are the temples?" I was in awe. These inhabitants of Muktinath were completely ignorant of the existence of the sacred sites. In the distance I could hear the sound of two other women who sat under a stone arch holding mala, Buddhist beads, as they prayed. I ran to them, assuming they would know the location of my destination because they were chanting, but it was no use. Neither one had ever even heard of the sacred flames.

Inhabitants of "Muktinath" were unaware of the sacred sites!

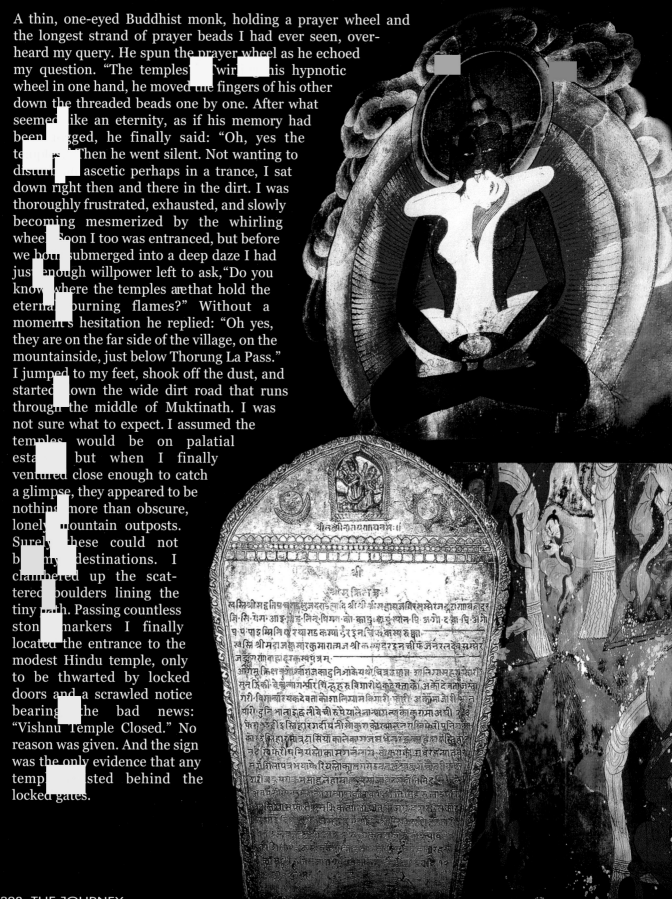

A thin, one-eyed Buddhist monk, holding a prayer wheel and the longest strand of prayer beads I had ever seen, overheard my query. He spun the prayer wheel as he echoed my question. "The temples?" Twirling his hypnotic wheel in one hand, he moved the fingers of his other down the threaded beads one by one. After what seemed like an eternity, as if his memory had been jogged, he finally said: "Oh, yes the temples." Then he went silent. Not wanting to disturb the ascetic perhaps in a trance, I sat down right then and there in the dirt. I was thoroughly frustrated, exhausted, and slowly becoming mesmerized by the whirling wheel. Soon I too was entranced, but before we both submerged into a deep daze I had just enough willpower left to ask, "Do you know where the temples are that hold the eternal burning flames?" Without a moment's hesitation he replied: "Oh yes, they are on the far side of the village, on the mountainside, just below Thorung La Pass." I jumped to my feet, shook off the dust, and started down the wide dirt road that runs through the middle of Muktinath. I was not sure what to expect. I assumed the temples would be on palatial estates, but when I finally ventured close enough to catch a glimpse, they appeared to be nothing more than obscure, lonely mountain outposts. Surely these could not be my destinations. I clambered up the scattered boulders lining the tiny path. Passing countless stone markers I finally located the entrance to the modest Hindu temple, only to be thwarted by locked doors and a scrawled notice bearing the bad news: "Vishnu Temple Closed." No reason was given. And the sign was the only evidence that any temple existed behind the locked gates.

A one-eyed
Buddhist priest
spins a prayer
wheel

Muktinath's
Iwalla Mai
Buddhist
temple:
interior murals
and exterior
stone tabletv

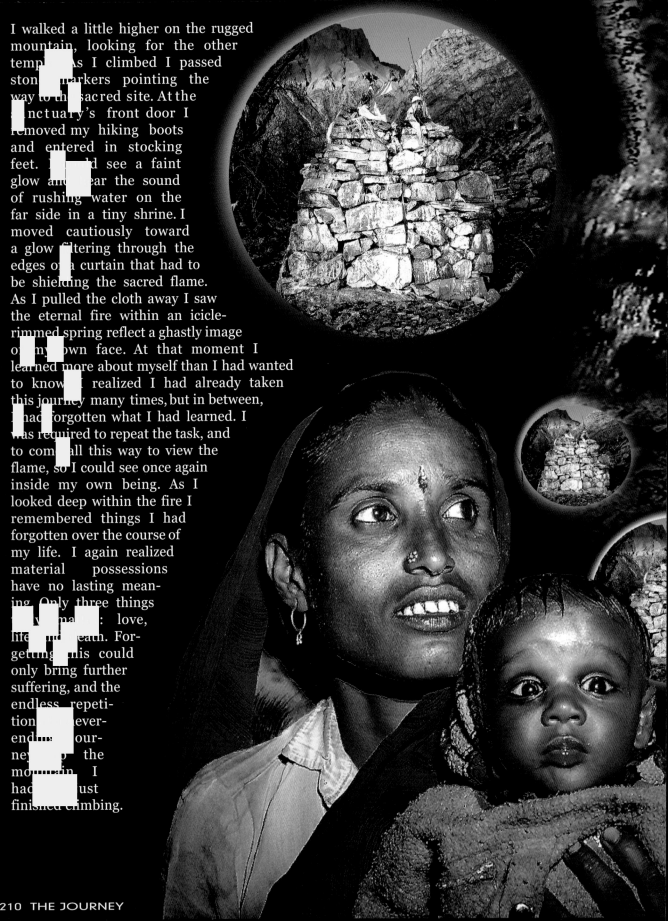

I walked a little higher on the rugged mountain, looking for the other temple. As I climbed I passed stone markers pointing the way to the sacred site. At the sanctuary's front door I removed my hiking boots and entered in stocking feet. I could see a faint glow and hear the sound of rushing water on the far side in a tiny shrine. I moved cautiously toward a glow filtering through the edges of a curtain that had to be shielding the sacred flame. As I pulled the cloth away I saw the eternal fire within an icicle-rimmed spring reflect a ghastly image of my own face. At that moment I learned more about myself than I had wanted to know. I realized I had already taken this journey many times, but in between, I had forgotten what I had learned. I was required to repeat the task, and to come all this way to view the flame, so I could see once again inside my own being. As I looked deep within the fire I remembered things I had forgotten over the course of my life. I again realized material possessions have no lasting mean- ing. Only three things truly matter: love, life and death. For- getting this could only bring further suffering, and the endless repeti- tion of a never- ending jour- ney up the mountain I had just finished climbing.

The natural eternal
flame at the
Iwalla Mai
Buddhist temple,
Muktinath

PEOPLE ON

"KUMARI:" THE VIRGINAL GODDESS CELEBRATED AN OLD MAN'S BIRTHDAY

THE SADHU WHO WRAPPED HIS TESTICLES AROUND A BROOM STICK

THE HOLY MAN WHO ASKED ME TO WASH DISHES IN THE GANGES RIVER

THE INDIAN BABAS WHO RIFFLED MY POCKETS AT A "SHIVARATRI" FESTIVAL

"DR. NOSE RING" WAS NOT A TRIBESMAN, HE CAME FROM NEW YORK CITY

THE SADHU WHO SAT IN A CIRCLE OF SMOKING COW DUNG FOR 17 YEARS

THE JOURNEY

THE YOUNG VENDER WHO SOLD H.I.V. "CURES" AND STATUES THAT "STOP" BULLETS

"PRIYA" ASKED TO HAVE A DEAD YAK'S HEAD CARRIED UP A LADDER

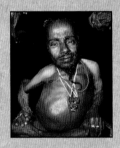

THE DEFORMED NUDE MIDGET BABA WHO OFFERED CHILUMS OF HASH

THE SNAKE CHARMER WHO WAS STONED TO DEATH

"BABU MARAJ" THE PRIEST I PLAYED DRUMS WITH UNTIL I PASSED BLOOD

"SHUSHAT" THE BUDDHIST MONK WHO TAUGHT ME HOW TO MEDITATE

SHIVA

Shiva is could be considered one of the most important and the most popular Hindu deity. Embodying many contradictions, he is the god of destruction and creation, as well as death and regeneration. Both feminine and masculine, he transcends all polarities.

The god of asceticism: Shiva is frequently depicted naked and smeared in cremation ash. From his long matted hair springs the sacred river of the Ganges. Deep in meditation with half-closed eyes, Shiva is also the god of fertility that controls the movements of the universe. His male aspect is conveyed by the symbol of the "Lingam", while his female energy is made manifest in the "Yoni".

Considered the master of yogis: it is in this guise that Saddhus hope to resemble Shiva's manifestation. The allegiances of Saddhus can be detected in the different markings they exhibit on their foreheads, torso, and arms. There are certain rivalries between different factions of Saddhus that have led to conflicts in the past, but ultimately all Saddhus come from the same root.

RELIGION

Saddhus are worshipped as living gods. Practitioners believe that, when they catch sight of a Saddhu, a spark of spiritual energy is transmitted. Many followers give donations to Saddhus with the hope of receiving spiritual rewards in return. Saddhus renounce materialism and therefore have little or no monetary income other than the donations they receive from worshippers who seek the Saddhu's blessings.

There are many different sects and orders of Saddhus. Initiate trainee Saddhus, who embark on the spiritual path followed by Holy Men, symbolically die after renouncing materialism while simultaneously being reborn into spiritualism. A recognizable symbol of an initiate's rebirth is his shaven head covered by cremation ash.

Any reference to a novice's former life is considered irrelevant and his age and birthday in effect is reckoned from the point he gives up his former life. Each novice has a teacher, or guru, who acts as father, mother and teacher. The guru is the "dispeller of darkness" and pierces the "Veil of Illusion". In turn, the novice worships the guru as a manifestation of the divine, and makes every effort to satisfy him. The majority of Saddhus are considered moderate but sects can exhibit extremely radical behavior.

NAGA or "WARRIOR ASCETICS"

Most Saddhus sects are temperate, but the "Naga (naked) Babas", who are also referred to as "warrior ascetics", have no fear of death. They have existed since prehistoric times and are known to be extremely militant when waging war, not only on rival Saddhu sects, but also with Muslims and even British troops.

The Nagas have a formidable array of weapons — sticks, spears, swords, and, above all, tridents — although now these weapons have only a symbolic significance.

GORAKHNATHIS or JOGIS

The term Yogi (or Jogi) is a familiar one to most Westerners, although these Saddhus are also referred to as Gorakhnathis and "Nath Babas". They are followers of the "Tantric Way" as taught by the founder of the sect, Goraknath, rather than the Vedantic teachings of the eighth century philosopher, Shankara. They are devotees of Shiva in his manifestation as Bhairava. Goraknath, who has many temples dedicated to him, is considered an incarnation of Shiva, and therefore is worshipped as a deity by the Yogis.

UDASIN

The Udasin sect was founded in the sixteenth century by Shrichandra, a son of Guru Nanak who was the founder of Sikhism. Hence, originally, this too was a Sikh sect. The Udasin are also known as the Nanakputras ("followers of Nanak"), and they respect the teachings of the Grantha Saheb: the sacred texts of Sikhism.

The Udasin were excommunicated however by Guru Nanak's successor and subsequently turned to Hinduism. They worship Panchayatana, a deity that comprises five separate deities: Shiva, Vishnu, the Sun, Durga, and Ganesh; but their founder, Shrichandra is still recognized and considered spiritually powerful. In essence, the Udasin now resemble the Shaiva Sannyasis.

NAGA BABAS

SHIVA BABAS

NAGA BABAS

AGHORIS

The Aghoris is now a small and obscure sect, although for thousands of years they were extremely powerful and prolific. Practicing radical deprivation and extreme sacrifice the Aghoris worship Lord Shiva as the Conqueror of Death. The Aghoris are nomads but frequently dwell temporally at cremation sites. Unlike other Saddhus, who attempt to achieve Enlightenment through abstinence, the Aghoris believe that a reversal of such practices can actually speed up the process of "Transcendence" and as a result they eat meat and drink alcohol, which is castigated by the majority of other Saddhu sects.

Extreme ritual practices are attributed to the Aghoris, such as eating the putrid flesh of cremated humans, consuming feces and urine from dogs, using human skulls as drinking vessels and meditating while seated on a corpse. Whether such practices occur today is in dispute, but it is certainly true that Aghoris surround themselves with artifacts of death. Some question if the Aghoris' sacrifices exist, but it is certain, at least in a ritual context, as a type of "eucharist", that some of these cannibalistic "inhuman" acts are still practiced.

RAMANANDIS

The ascetic Ramananda founded the sect Ramananda Sampradaya, which is also known as Ramanandis, at the beginning of the fourteenth century. It is an offshoot of the school of philosophy founded by the Vaishnava teacher Ramanuja (1017–1137). Ramananda selected Rama and Sita for his personal devotion and encouraged his followers to worship them as the central feature of the sect's religious practice. The Ramanandis sect has since evolved and changed, though it officially is still part of the Shri Sampradaya.

LAW AND KARMA

The legal system of India is unique it that it embodies an essential conflict which does not exist in Western politics and law. Church and state in the West have evolved in parallel but separate arenas, but India, being a vast and culturally diverse region, practices an ancient, metaphysical, and Byzantine type of legal system, upon which the British attempted to impose its own form of legal system during the period of the Raj in the nineteenth century.

The indigenous religious faiths deal with such metaphysical matters as life, death, and rebirth. The secular state, on the other hand, attempts to dispense justice on a local, state, and federal level within a system grounded in Western values rooted in common law. Although modeled after England's legal system, whereas in Britain the constitution is fluid and laws are constantly being updated and changed, the weight of bureaucracy engendered by such a large region as the Indian subcontinent has engendered very few substantial legal revisions since the Raj. Viewed as a whole, the Indian judicial system, because it has not been continually modified, has severely impeded commerce, economic advances, and political unity.

The system's most powerful entity is the Supreme Court in New Delhi. Indian courts have jurisdiction over most economic and political transactions. They have the authority to issue directives, orders, and writs, as well as having powers of enforcement. The president of India appoints judges to the court, who serve until the age of sixty-five. At the state level are the High Courts; because they are the most powerful legal entity within each individual Indian state, they consequently have immediate power over any subordinate court within their jurisdiction.

HINDU LAW

HINDU CANON

By Western standards Hinduism cannot be defined as a religion, because it lacks a formal linear structure and accommodates a staggering number of individual sects. However, there are certain principles that are followed by the majority of Hindus. At its center is Brahman, the Ultimate Reality, the union that is sought. Linked to Brahma is the concept of the Soul, or Atman, which is the animating energy in any living creature. The material world itself is but an illusion. Brahma is the creator of the world, including the deities that individual sects worship. A fundamental idea is that of rebirth. On death, the soul is reborn as an animal, human being, or heavenly body. The effect of one's actions in life ("Karma") determine one's status in the next. This cycle of life is known as Samsara, and it is the goal of all to achieve liberation from this ("Moksha").

CASTE SYSTEM

Many Westerners question the ancient, deeply entrenched Indian caste system, and the frequent moral conflicts that ensue between it and the Western style legal system under which the subcontinent is governed. The caste "class" system is intimately bound to important Hindu religious doctrines that can overshadow the power of India's legal system. The strict caste system, condoned by thousands of years of Hindu tradition, classifies groups of people into specific inescapable categories, and is considered more important than most institutionalized law for the majority of India's population. The most significant rule of the caste system dictates that people within a social caste, or class, can only marry within that caste, which makes each class inclusive and, as a result, renders social mobility virtually impossible.

Each individual caste has its own traditional behaviors, myths, occupations, and even diet. The castes are arranged in a hierarchy: members of the lowest caste are referred to as the "Untouchables", as those of the highest are referred to as "Brahmans".

India's caste system does not exactly correlate, although it is similar in nature to the Western classification system. The most significant difference is, however, that in the West it is possible, and even encouraged, to move either "up or down" from a higher class to a lower class or within a specific class, while on the other hand India's caste system makes it impossible to evolve out of any one caste into another. Hindu doctrine dictates that caste status is deemed to be the result of Karma: one's place in society has been predetermined by one's actions in a former life, and does not suggest the possibility of changing castes within one's present lifetime. To achieve a higher status in the next life, it is necessary to accept one's present station.

The majority of Hindu marriages are arranged by people who are interested in the future welfare of the couple because a successful marriage within any caste is believed to result in release from the wheel of life and rebirth. The search for a suitable spouse usually takes considerable time to safeguard family unity and to assure future prosperity because it is necessary for the bride to practice similar religious, cultural, and financial traditions as the groom.

Once a suitable match has been found, an auspicious day for the marriage is chosen. Traditionally, weddings take place at the bride's home, but now more public venues are often preferred. The time dedicated to any given wedding, and the associated rituals, varies; some last as long as four or five days, though modern weddings are generally shorter. The actual wedding ceremony is accompanied by the various traditional rituals that involve sacred texts recitals in the archaic language of Sanskrit.

At the conclusion of the public ceremony the bride and groom go to their new home and begin married life with a series of private rituals. In a sense, a Hindu's entire married life is considered to be a ritual, in which childbirth and child rearing play a very important role that only ends with the death of either the husband or wife.

CONCLUSION

Deep underlying truths are carried away when we pursue an experience of self knowledge. This is something we can understand, even if we are not all actively struggling toward that goal. The quest is quite literally a matter of life and death, for it seeks liberation from the eternal cycle of extinction, but in order to achieve this state of freedom from suffering and desire, it is necessary to pass through this world and to perform extraordinary acts of penance and self-abnegation.

A Hindu wise man described the difference between one who searches for knowledge and one who has already attained it: "The man of knowledge perceives everything with senses withdrawn; the man who has transcended knowledge, when dealing with the world, sees himself as part of being. His senses and mind function in response to events in the world, but his "Self" does not identify with his body and mind."

Rather than question the many paths to a common goal, we might take the word of one sage who assured me when I reach the place I am seeking, I will not have to worry about understanding it; I will know I have arrived. We are all seeking knowledge and understanding of the unknown. We will understand, and can reach, a higher awareness. I am convinced it is possible to transcend physical reality and for us to achieve a complete understanding of the universe.

When Westerners encounter rich cultures, religions and philosophies, it is as if they are tapping into a deep ancient reservoir of knowledge and experience. Enormous differences in cultures seem to vanish when we focus on a higher reality. Indeed, it is the very differences in our cultures that ensure we are really human beings, uniquely incarnate in the world and within time. These differences require an open mind, and an open heart to understand and accept, but in so doing, we can overcome the intolerance that plagues our modern world.

In the transcendent view of reality, all of us are on parallel paths to the same destination; it is only human vanity and illusion of separation that gives rise to the false values of religious conflict. If we are truly to overcome our growing fear and the prospect of conflagration, we must understand what wisdom can teach us: the world is already on fire, destroying and renewing itself in every minute of our existence. To escape the fire, we have to overcome anxiety, becalm the senses, and plunge headlong into the greater acceptance of all cultures, so as to be able to understand what now is inexplicable, but still within our grasp, beneath the surface of all reality.

BIBLIOGRAPHY

A.C. Bhaktivedanta Swami Prabhupada. : Bhagavad-gita As It Is : MacMillan 1972.

Agrawala, Vasudeva Sharana. Gupta art : a history of Indian art : Prakashan, 1977

Anand, Kewal Krishna. Indian philosophy : the concept of Karma : Asia Books 1982.

Anand, Mulk Raj. 1905- The Hindu view of art. : Asia House 1957

Anand, Mulk Raj. Kama kala : the basis of Hindu sculpture : New York Nagel, 1962.

Balbir Singh. 1930- Hindu ethics : the concept of God : Humanities Press, 1984.

Banerjea, Jitendra Nath, Hindu iconography : University of Calcutta, 1941.

Beck, L. Adams, The splendour of Asia New York, Dodd / Mead 1926

Bernard, Theos, Penthouse of the gods : Scribner's 1939.

Berry, Thomas Mary, Buddhism : New York, Hawthorn Books, 1966.

Bhagavad-gita : Krishna's counsel in time of war, New York : Bantam Books, 1986.

Blackie, John Stuart, The natural history of atheism, London : Daldy, Isbister, 1877

Blofeld, John. The Tantric Mysticism of Tibet, New York: Causeway Books, 1974.

Bowes, Pratima. Hindu intellectual tradition, Columbia, Mo. : South Asia Books, c1977.

Boyd, Doug. Swami, New York : Random House with Robert Briggs l976

Brown, W. Norman. "Hinduism". Encyclopedia Americana, 1995. Vol 7.

The Buddha, New York, N.Y. : Thames and Hudson, 1996.

Buddhism : art and faith / edited by W. Zwalf, New York : Macmillan, c1985.

Buddhism : the illustrated guide : Oxford University Press, 2001.

Clarke, Peter B. The World's Religions : Marshall Limited, 1993.

Coomaraswamy, Ananda Kentish, Gospel of Buddhism, Harper & Row 1964

Coomaraswamy, Ananda Kentish, Hinduism and Buddhism, Greenwood Press 1971

Corless, Roger. The vision of Buddhism : Paragon House, 1989.

Corlett, William. The Buddha way N.Y. : Bradbury Press, 1980,

Coward, Harold G. Hindu ethics : University of New York Press, 1989.

Crawford, S. Cromwell. Dilemmas of Hindu ethics : North American University 1995

David-Neel, Alexandra. Buddhism, doctrines and its methods : St. Martin's Press, 1978.

Deneck, Marguerite-Marie. Indian Art London : Paul Hamlyn, 1967.

Embree, Ainslie Thomas. The Hindu tradition : Modern Library 1966

Enders, Gordon Bandy. Foreign devil : Simon and Schuster, 1942.

Engaged Buddhist reader, Berkeley : Parallax Press, 1996.

Fingesten, Peter. East is East : Philidelphia, Muhlenberg Press 1956

Forbes, Geraldine Hancock. Positivism in Bengal Colombia, South Asia Books, 1975

Gach, Gary. The complete idiot's guide to understanding Buddhism : Alpha, 2002.

Gard, Richard Abbott. 1914- Buddhism : New York, G. Braziller, 1961.

Gopinatha Rao, T. A. 1872-1919. Elements of Hindu iconography : Law Printing 1914

Goswamy, B.N. Essence of Indian Art. Asian Art Museum of San Francisco, 1986.

Grimm, George. 1868-1945. The doctrine of the Buddha : Akademie-Verlag, 1958.

Gudmunsen, Chris. Wittgenstein and Buddhism New York : Barnes & Noble Books, 1977

Hartsuiker, Dolf. Sadhus : India's mystic holy men American Distribution Corp.1993.

Heimann, Betty. 1888-1961. Facets of Indian thought. London, Allen & Unwin 1964

Hopkins, Edward Washburn. 1857-1932. Ethics of India : Yale University Press, 1924.

Humphreys, Christmas,The way of action;philosophy for Western life : Macmillan, 1960.

Hutchinson, John A. Paths of Faith : New York:McGraw-Hill, l975.

Ikeda, Daisaku. Buddhism, the first millennium New York : Harper & Row, 1977.

Jacobson, Nolan Pliny. Buddhism the religion of analysis Carbondale : S. Illinois U. 1970

Kerouac, Jack. 1922-1969. Some of the Dharma, New York : Viking, 1997.
Kim, Young Oon. 1915- India's religious quest New York : Golden Gate Pub. Co., 1976.
Kirk, James A. Stories of the Hindus : New York, Macmillan 1972
Klostermaier, Klaus K. 1933- Buddhism : a short introduction Oxford : Oneworld, 1999.
Kramrisch, Stella. 1898- Exploring India's sacred art : U. of Pennsylvania Press, 1983.
Kramrisch, Stella. The Art of India Through the Ages.London: Phaidon Press, 1965.
Krishnamurti, J. (Jiddu), 1895- Commentaries on living : New York, Harper 1960
Krom, N. J, Thorson's principles of Buddhism, London : Thorsons, 1996.
Lacy, Creighton. The conscience of India; traditions in the modern world : Holt 1965
Lingat, Robert. The Classic Law of India : University of California Press, 1973.
Lopez, Donald S. 1952- The story of Buddhism : Harper San Francisco, 2001.
Lowenstein, Tom. The vision of the Buddha : path to enlightenment Duncan Baird, 2000
Masutani, Fumio. 1902- Buddha. Tokyo, Kadokawa-shoten, 1969.
Mehta, N. P. Glimpses of truth as they came to me Bombay : Hind Kitabs, 1953.
Melamed, Samuel Max, Spinoza and Buddha; visions of dead God, U. of Chicago1933
Menen, Aubrey. The Mystics. Photos. by Graham Hall. New York, Dial Press, 1974.
Mookerjee, Ajit. Ritual art of India New York : Thames and Hudson, 1985.
Morgan, Kenneth W. ed. The Religion of the Hindus.New York: The Ronald Press, 1953.
Nisker, Wes. Buddha's nature : a practical guide to the cosmos : Bantam Books, 2000
Organ, Troy Wilson. The self in Indian philosopy. The Hague : Mouton, 1964.
Organ, Troy Wilson. Third eye philosophy : Athens, Ohio : Ohio University Press1987
Palmer, Martin. Kuan Yin : myths and revelations London : Thorsons, 1995.
Powell, Andrew. 1957- Living Buddhism; New York : Harmony Books, c1989.
Prebish, Charles S. Buddhism--a modern perspective : Pennsylvania State1975
Radhakrishnan, S. (Sarvepalli), 1888-1975. Indian philosophy, Humanities Press, 1929
Rambach, Pierre. 1925- The golden age of Indian art : Studio Publications 1955
Ross, Nancy Wilson. 1901-1986. Buddhism, a way of life : Random House, 1980.
Ross, Nancy Wilson. 1901-1986. Three ways of Asian wisdom : Simon and Schuster 1966
Schuon, Frithjof, Treasures of Buddhism : World Wisdom Books, 1993.
Shah, K. T. (Khushal Talaksi) The splendour that was India; Bombay,Taraporevala1930
Shearer, Alistair. The Hindu vision, New York : Thames and Hudson, 1993.
Shedlock, Marie L, Eastern stories and legends, E.P. Dutton & Company, 1920
Snellgrove, David. Indo-Tibetan Buddhism. Boston: Shambala Press,1987, Vol. 1.
Snelling, John. 1943- The Buddhist handbook American International Distribution 1991
Snelling, John. 1943- The elements of Buddhism Shaftesbury, Dorset : Element, 1996
Story, Francis. Collected writings Anagarika Sugatananda. : Buddhist Society, 1973
Strong, John. 1948- The Buddha : a short biography Oxford : Oneworld, 2001.
Stutterheim, Willem Frederik, Indian influences in old-Balinese art : India Society, 1935
Suzuki, Daisetz Teitaro, The essence of Buddhism Los Alamitos, CA : Xuan Thu, 1990
Teachings of the Hindu mystics / edited by Andrew Harvey, Shambhala/ Random 2001
Upanishads. English. The thirteen principal Upanishads from Sanskrit, Oxford U. 1971
Vivekananda, Swami, Teachings of Swami Vivekananda : Advaita Ashrama 1964
Watters, Thomas, On Yuan Chwang's travels in India, 629-645 A.D. Royal Asiatic,1904
Watts, Alan, 1915-1973. Buddhism, the religion of no-religion Boston : C.E. Tuttle, 1996
Watts, Alan, The early writings of Alan Watts : 1931-1938 : Calif. : Celestial Arts,1987
Wilson, H. H, Essays and lectures on the religion Hindus. London,1862.
The World of Buddhism : Buddhist monks and nuns in society N.Y. : Facts on File, 1984.
Wright, Arthur F. 1913-1976. Buddhism in Chinese history : Stanford Press, 1959.
Wright, Brooks. 1922- Interpreter of Buddhism to the West : N.Y. Bookman, 1957
Zimmer, Heinrich Robert, Philosophies of India; edited Joseph Campbell:Princeton 1969
Zimmer, Heinrich Robert, Myths and symbols in Indian art : Pantheon Books 1946

THE END IS THE BEGINNING THE BEGINNING IS THE END
THE BEGINNING IS THE END THE END IS THE BEGINNING
THE END IS THE BEGINNING THE BEGINNING IS THE END
THE BEGINNING IS THE END THE END IS THE BEGINNING

THE AUTHOR AND HIS PHOTOGRAPHIC MANDALA MURAL:
"ANALYSES OF REALITIES" AT SAN FRANCISCO'S
ART COMMISSION GALLERY: "CAPRICORN ASUNDER" 1973

© 2004 TASCHEN GmbH
Hohenzollernring 53, D–50672 Köln
www.taschen.com

Production: Print Company Verlagsgesellschaft mbH, Vienna

Printed in Italy
ISBN 3–8228–2806–8